Osanbashi pier, Yoko

12 July 20

The site offices of the architects, engineers and contractors of the new Yokohama International Port Terminal are located in a temporary building at the entrance of the pier. The third floor is shared by Foreign Office Architects and Structural Design Group.
Although most design work was done by FOA in a Tokyo downtown office, detail design continues here as the foundation work goes on outside.
Alejandro Zaera-Polo oversees a few decisions with an engineer of SDG and an architect of FOA.
Farshid Moussavi opens the window to their building site.

年(YEAR)				2000							
年度(FINANCIAL YEAR)	平成11年度(HEISEI 11TH)										平成12年度(H
月(MONTH)	1月 JAN.	2月 FEB.	3月 MAR.	4月 APR.	5月 MAY	6月 JUN.	7月 JUL.	8月 AUG.	9月 SEP.	10月 OCT.	11 NO
準備工事 PREPARETION						◎着工 COMMENCEMENT					
杭工事 PILING WORK											
根切工事 EXCAVATION											
地下躯体工事 UNDERGROUND STRUCTURAL WORK											
地上部基礎・1Fスラブ躯体工事 FOUNDATION & GROND FLOOR SLAB											
プレストレス工事 PRE-STRESSED CONCRETE SLAB							シース管・PC鋼線挿入TUBE & PC WIRE INST				
地上部鉄骨工事 STEEL WORK(SUPER STRUCTURE)											
外部仕上工事 EXTENAL FINISHING WORK											
内部仕上工事 INTERNAL FINSHISHING WORK											
設備工事 MECHANICAL & ELECTRICAL WORK											
外構工事 EXTERNAL WORK											
竣工・引渡し COMPLETION & HANDOVER											
プロモーション工程(PROMOTION SCHEDULE)	1月 JAN.	2月 FEB.	3月 MAR.	4月 APR.	5月 MAY	6月 JUN.	7月 JUL.	8月 AUG.	9月 SEP.	10月 OCT.	11 NO
鋼管杭 STEEL PILING WORK	業者決定 施工図 承認 製作										
スラブ床版 PRE-STRESSED CONCRETE SLAB		業者決定 施工図 承認 製作									
プレストレス PRE-STRESSING		業者決定 施工図 承認 製作									
鉄骨メインガーダー STEEL MAIN GARDER	ステップ解析 STEP ANALYSIS		施工図 承認		業者決定 製作図 納まり検討 承認					製作	
2F・RF折板 1ST FLOOR & ROOF STEEL FOLDING CONST.	ステップ解析 STEP ANALYSIS		施工図 承認	業者決定 製作図			納まり検討			承認	
ウッドデッキ(外部) WOOD DECK(EXTERNAL)											
ウッドデッキ(内部) WOOD DECK(INTERNAL)											
外装建具 EXTERNAL GLASS & SASH						ステップ解析 STEP ANALYSIS				業者決定	
内装建具(スチール・ステンレス・木製) INTERNAL SASH(STEEL/STAINLESS STEEL/WOOD)											
タイル・石 TILE & STONE											
躯体図(1期工事) FORMWORK DRAWING (PHASE-1)				作図	承認						
総合図(1期工事) GENERAL LAYOUT (A+S+M+E) (PHASE-1)				作図	承認						
躯体図(2期工事) FORMWORK DRAWING (PHASE-2)								作図			
総合図(1期工事) GENERAL LAYOUT (A+S+M+E) (PHASE-2)						作図		承認			
平面詳細図 DETAIL DRAWING FOR PLAN											作
天井伏せ図 CEILING PLAN		総合図(1期)PHASE-1	承認								
(設備施工図) WORKING DRAWING FOR M&E					総合図(2期)PHASE-2		承認	施工図	承認		
各種部会 RESEARCH WORKING GROPE	1月 JAN.	2月 FEB.	3月 MAR.	4月 APR.	5月 MAY	6月 JUN.	7月 JUL.	8月 AUG.	9月 SEP.	10月 OCT.	11 NO
鉄骨部会(メインガーダー・折版) STEEL SECTION		基本検討 BASIC			詳細検討 DETAIL RESEARCH						
PC部会(PC版・プレストレス) PC SLAB PRE-STRESSING SECTION		基本検討BASIC RESEARCH			詳細検討 DETAIL RESEARCH						
カーテンウォール部会 CURTAIN WALL SECTION		基本検討 BASIC RESEARCH			詳細検討 DETAIL RESEARCH						
仕上げ部会(ウッドデッキ) FINSHING WORK(WOOD DECK)SECTION		基本検討 BASIC RESEARCH				詳細検討 DETAIL RESEARCH					
防水部会 WATERPROOFING SECTION		基本検討 BASIC RESEARCH			詳細検討 DETAIL RESEARCH						
音響部会 ACOUSTIC SECTION		基本検討 BASIC			詳細検討 DETAIL RESEARCH						
設備部会 ELECTRICAL & MECHANICAL SECTION		基本検討 BASIC RESEARCH			詳細検討 DETAIL RESEARCH						
3次元CAD・施工図部会 3D CAD SECTION		基本検討 BASIC RESEARCH			詳細検討 DETAIL RESEARCH						

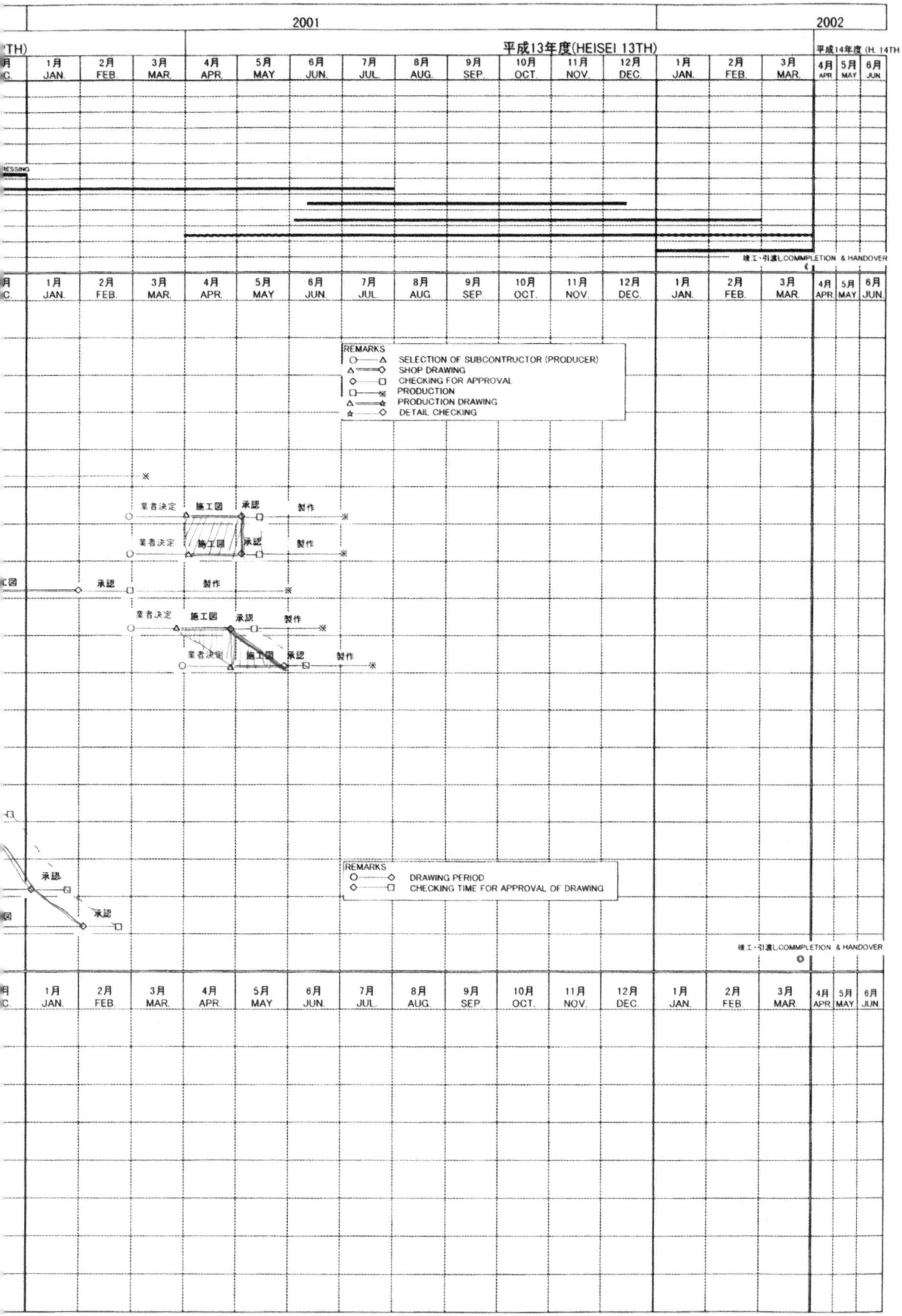

TH)							平成13年度(HEISEI 13TH)							平成14年度 (H. 14TH		
月 IC.	1月 JAN.	2月 FEB.	3月 MAR.	4月 APR.	5月 MAY	6月 JUN.	7月 JUL.	8月 AUG.	9月 SEP.	10月 OCT.	11月 NOV.	12月 DEC.	1月 JAN.	2月 FEB.	3月 MAR.	4月 5月 6月 APR MAY JUN.

RESSING

竣工・引渡L.COMMPLETION & HANDOVER

月 IC.	1月 JAN.	2月 FEB.	3月 MAR.	4月 APR.	5月 MAY	6月 JUN.	7月 JUL.	8月 AUG.	9月 SEP.	10月 OCT.	11月 NOV.	12月 DEC.	1月 JAN.	2月 FEB.	3月 MAR.	4月 5月 6月 APR MAY JUN.

REMARKS
- ○——△ SELECTION OF SUBCONTRACTOR (PRODUCER)
- △——◇ SHOP DRAWING
- ◇——□ CHECKING FOR APPROVAL
- □——✕ PRODUCTION
- △——☆ PRODUCTION DRAWING
- ☆——◇ DETAIL CHECKING

業者決定 施工図 承認 製作

業者決定 施工図 承認 製作

C図 承認 製作

業者決定 施工図 承認 製作

業者決定 施工図 承認 製作

承認

承認

REMARKS
- ○——◇ DRAWING PERIOD
- ◇——□ CHECKING TIME FOR APPROVAL OF DRAWING

竣工・引渡L.COMMPLETION & HANDOVER

月 IC.	1月 JAN.	2月 FEB.	3月 MAR.	4月 APR.	5月 MAY	6月 JUN.	7月 JUL.	8月 AUG.	9月 SEP.	10月 OCT.	11月 NOV.	12月 DEC.	1月 JAN.	2月 FEB.	3月 MAR.	4月 5月 6月 APR MAY JUN.

Welcome to Yokohama

Yokohama is a bustling city with a population of more than 3 million people, making it Japan's second largest city after metropolitan Tokyo. Yokohama's modern history dates from 1859, when the port was opened to the international community. In the more than 130 years since then, Yokohama has continued to serve as an important gateway between Japan and world, while also playing a central role in Japan's modernization and internationalization.

Yokohama is also taking on a more prominent role internationally. Nowhere is this more apparent than in the citizens of Yokohama themselves, who are noted for their openness and progressiveness. Their vitality enhances this city's unique personality, making Yokohama an appealing place to live and work.

Yokohama is continually working toward a better future and has set its sights firmly on the twenty-first century by pushing ahead with urban development. Yokohama's comprehensive urban plan seeks to integrate various sectors of the community, including local and international business.

Yokohama is an ideal business location with well built infrastructure, as well as abundant greenery and an attractive living environment. The city also boasts administrative facilities befitting a major center in addition to the superb integration of research, service, and high-tech sectors. This provides an ideal environment for the effective execution of business activities and research development.

I hope you will take time to gain a better understanding of Yokohama's many attractions. Furthermore I also encourage you to visit Yokohama and consider setting up operations here.

Dr. Hidenobu Takahide, Mayor City of Yokohama
http://www.city.yokohama.jp/welcome/indexE.html

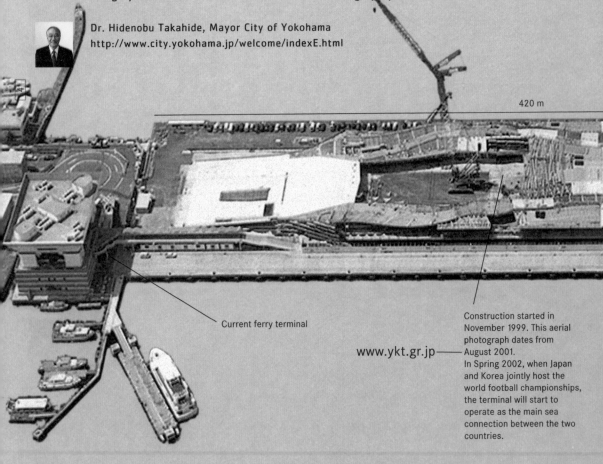

420 m

Current ferry terminal

www.ykt.gr.jp

Construction started in November 1999. This aerial photograph dates from August 2001.
In Spring 2002, when Japan and Korea jointly host the world football championships, the terminal will start to operate as the main sea connection between the two countries.

Groundbreaking ceremony. http://www.2ken.motnet.go.jp/ne0005100/news04.html

Since Foreign Office Architects won the competition for the new Yokohama International Port Terminal in 1995, the project has been taking shape and changing shapes in a close collaboration between architects, engineers, contractors and client.
This process is played back in the following pages of Verb.

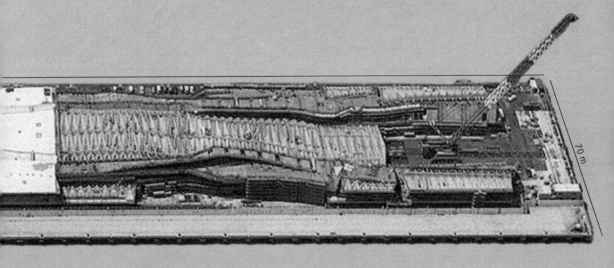

70 m

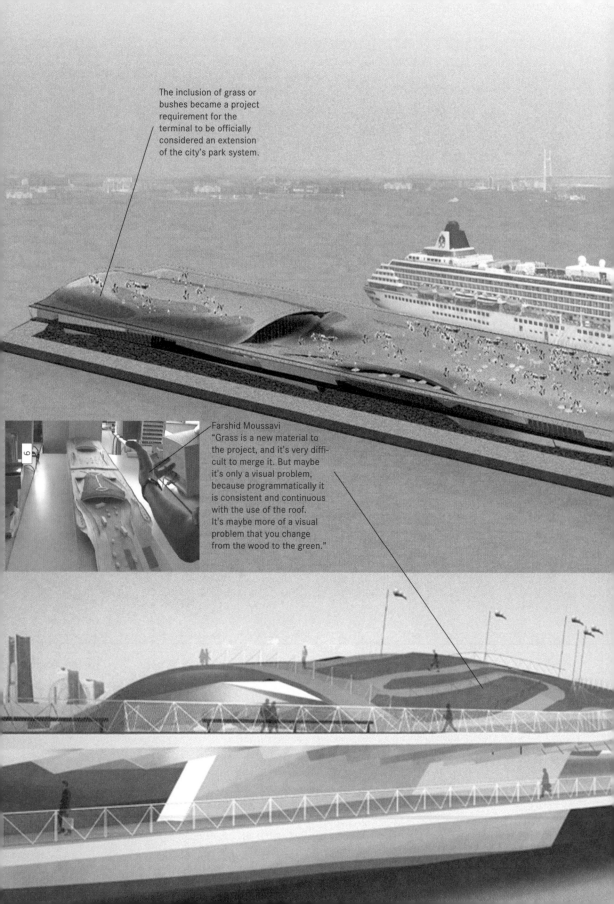

The inclusion of grass or bushes became a project requirement for the terminal to be officially considered an extension of the city's park system.

Farshid Moussavi
"Grass is a new material to the project, and it's very difficult to merge it. But maybe it's only a visual problem, because programmatically it is consistent and continuous with the use of the roof. It's maybe more of a visual problem that you change from the wood to the green."

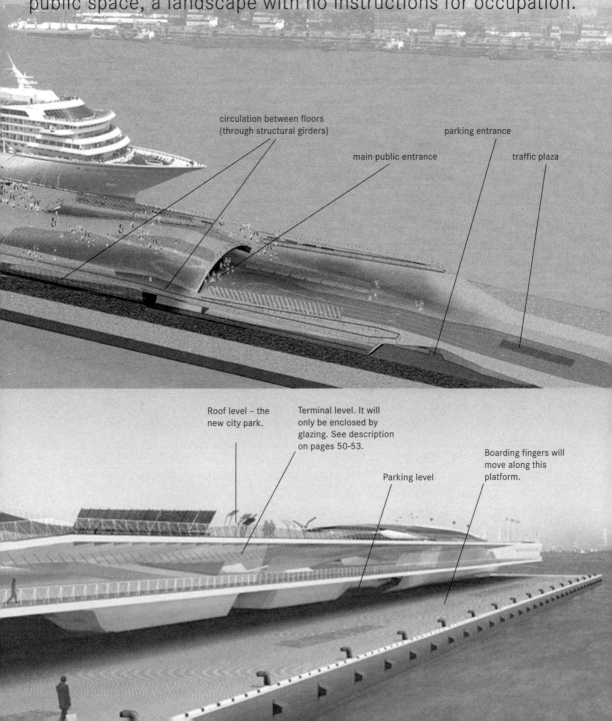

FOA (1995) > Our proposal for the new terminal will be a mediating device between the system of public spaces of Yokohama and the management of the cruise passenger flow. The components are used as a device of reciprocal de-territorialization: a public space that wraps around the terminal, and a functional structure which becomes the mould of an a-typological public space, a landscape with no instructions for occupation.

circulation between floors
(through structural girders)

parking entrance

main public entrance

traffic plaza

Roof level – the
new city park.

Terminal level. It will
only be enclosed by
glazing. See description
on pages 50-53.

Parking level

Boarding fingers will
move along this
platform.

FOA (1995) > Using the ground surface to create a complementary public space to Yamashita Park, our proposal will result in the first perpendicular penetration of the urban space within Yokohama Bay. The ground of the city will be seamlessly connected to the boarding level, and from there it will bifurcate to produce a multiplicity of urban events.

While the patches of green will give the roof its "park" character, the undulating wood surface will allow for different types of public appropriation and for the celebration of big public events.

FOA's Lluís Viu stands next to the prototype of the handrail which will be used throughout the building with some variations. He is looking out from the roof of their former Tokyo office.

YOKOHAMA INTERNATIONAL PORT TERMINAL
<u>Cost</u>: € 25.100.000.000 / ¥ 232.407.407. <u>Building area</u>: 43.843 m². <u>Competition</u>: 1995. <u>Completion date</u>: 29 noviembre 2002.
<u>Client</u>: The City of Yokohama. <u>Competition. Design team</u>: Farshid Moussavi, Alejandro Zaera-Polo, Iván Ascanio, Yoon King Chong,
Michael Cosmas, Jung-Hyun Hwang, Guy Westbrook. <u>Engineering advisors</u>: Ove Arup & Partners. <u>Basic Design Stage 1</u>: Farshid Moussavi,
Alejandro Zaera-Polo, Felix Bendito, Jordi Mansilla, Kenichi Matsuzawa, Santiago Triginer. <u>Basic Design Stage 2</u>: Farshid Moussavi,
Alejandro Zaera-Polo, Victoria Castillejos, Dafne Gil, Kenichi Matsuzawa, Oriol Montfort, Xavier Ortiz, Lluís Viu, José Saenz, Julián Varas,
Thomasine Wolfensberger. <u>Detail design and supervision</u>: Farshid Moussavi, Alejandro Zaera-Polo, Kensuke Kishikawa, Yasuhisa Kikuchi,
Izumi Kobayashi, Kenichi Matsuzawa, Tomofomi Nagayama, Xavier Ortiz, Lluís Viu, Keisuke Tamura. <u>Local architects</u>: GKK Architects.
<u>Structural engineers</u>: Structural Design Group (SDG). <u>Mechanical and electrical engineers</u>: P.T. Morimura.

Paper model of the roof folds
made by Kunio Watanabe (SDG)

ANNOUNCEMENT FROM THE CITY OF YOKOHAMA: GROUNDBREAKING CEREMONY
March 30, 2000, at 11:30. Osanbashi Pier
Construction of the Yokohama Osanbashi International Passenger Ship Terminal, the gateway to Yokohama in the 21st century, will soon begin. The new terminal features a fashionable wavy roof with inventive curved lines and beam-free interior spaces. The city's mayor, Hidenobu Takahide and the designers will attend the groundbreaking ceremony. The new terminal is scheduled for completion in the spring of 2002, in time for the soccer World Cup.
The Star Cruise ship company (head office: Singapore) will begin regular cruise service in and out of this new terminal on The Super Star Leo (76,800 tons), one of the largest passenger ships in Asia.

ROLLERCOASTER CONSTRUCTION

ALEJANDRO ZAERA-POLO

This article describes the work process and collaborations that have marked the development of the terminal's design concept. There's a jump from page 18 to page 33 in order to incorporate the engineer Kunio Watanabe's vision of the evolution of the structural concept.

"This is where amateurs have an advantage over pros. A pro knows what he can deliver, and rarely goes beyond it. An amateur has no concept of his limitations and generally goes beyond them."

Trey Gunn, "Road Diaries", Project Two. Discipline Global Mobile 1998

Architecture is not a plastic art, but the engineering of material life. Despite the classifications, architecture is a plastic problem only if you decide that plastic is your material. But that is just a particular case of architecture. This is what we hope distinguishes our work from other surface-complex architecture. We have grown tired of the associations with Saarinen, Utzon and Gehry, but despite the formal similarities, and our appreciation of their work, these comparisons are based purely on the formal output. Formal concerns are of significance, but this association does not tell the whole story. For example, Gehry works in exactly the opposite direction to us: he produces a spatial effect that is subsequently implemented by means of construction. He is primarily concerned with consistency in the spatial effects. The result may sometimes be similar, but the process of reaching it is radically different. What distinguishes the work we do from his is fundamentally the process, as our main priority is to produce consistency in the process of construction and material organisation. In fact, we are interested not in having preconceived effects, but rather in exploring the materials – and here we should understand material in the broadest sense – as a source of ideas and effects.

Processes are far more interesting than ideas. Ideas are linked to existing codes, operating critically or in alignment with pre-existing systems of ideas. Rather than making a project the implementation of an idea, or the scaffolding of an image, what we are interested in is constructing, engineering processes on different levels. A process is the generation of a micro-history of a project, a kind of specific narrative where the entity of the project forms in a sequence. If geological, biological or human history, for instance, have something to teach us it is that these processes of temporal formation produce organisations of a far higher complexity and sophistication than instantaneous ideas. This is perhaps the most important development brought by information technology to our practice: we can design, synthesise and proliferate specific histories, scripts for a project. Writing a project, like in Eisenman; introduce a sequential development rather than deploying a form, an image. Proliferate, wait for the emergence of the project. Writing code: Let's see what happens IF: We are no longer trapped in the traditional compulsion to reproduce historical models, or to invent them from scratch. We do not have to produce a project as a reproduction, a derivation or the invention of a historical model. We do not need to produce complexity by making collages: we can synthesise the processes of generation as a kind of accelerated motion, adding information integrally to the construction. This sequential, integrative addition produces more ambiguous effects, more capable of resonating on different levels than straightforward ideological statements, metaphors, allegories or reproductions.

Through our interests in the processes of construction and engineering of material life, we constantly get involved with all sorts of technologies. And techniques are always associated with performances, producing effects, delivering services. Technique has become the domain of architectural services; but architecture as a service industry is a deadly business and it rarely delivers interesting architecture. Jacques Herzog says that architects will have to become like the Spice Girls: soon, only star-architecture will be worth being involved with. The rest will be architectural services crap... But the concept of architectural services comes out of the coupling of architectural technology and effect: a good professional is capable of using the right techniques to produce the right effects. But what will happen if we divorce technique from service and effect? Is it possible to exploit the effective potential of architectural technique? This is where we think there may be an alternative to an architecture that masters effects; at least, a-priori effects... There is an enormous potential to be released, contained in the techniques of "architectural services", that has not been exploited in itself: project management, estimation, surveys, the modelling capacity of artificial intelligence... None of this stuff has been able to be integrated into the discipline of architecture, and this is leading the profession to bankruptcy: there are stars and there is architectural services... Complete schizophrenia. The real challenge is to exploit the potential of these technologies beyond their utilitarian association; integrate them into a discipline that has not evolved for a long time. Construct a new discipline out of them.

Talking of stars, we've never been pop enthusiasts. Pop is basically incompetent Afro-American music, packaged by image, concept, and life-style. Pop-stars rarely survive as musicians when the band dies, as their technical background is too weak to survive without the conceptual packaging and the image. We would rather be like Miles Davis. Jazz musicians usually have a more solid technical knowledge. They do not operate permanent organisations, but collaborate temporarily with other musicians in a variety of formations for specific projects. We can follow their lineage, witness the migration of techniques from Parker to Miles and from Miles to Corea, Zawinul, Coltrane... Of course, style cannot be discarded: it is impossible to operate without it. But would it be possible to generate style from technique? What is interesting about jazz formations and lineage is to see how personal styles evolve in the process. There are areas of stylistic stability, umbrellas that host drifters. Miles made some umbrellas, like Coleman, Coltrane and Zawinul did after being under his... Holland, Haden, Shorter, Brecker evolved through them and eventually created their own... Or they dissolved into other umbrellas without vanishing as musicians. And, as with architectural umbrellas, this process has nothing to do with marketing, management, timesheets, client portfolio, pension plans... It has to do with the production of knowledge, and it requires a very deep personal involvement from participants. In the production of a project of this nature, there is a very delicate balance against very powerful forces that threaten continuously to stratify the work, to turn it into a conventional process. If one does not take these forces into account, they may paralyse the project. If one is too obedient, they will destroy it.

Greedy consultants, managers who measure work in man hours and hours per drawing, and people by years of experience, mediocre client representatives that mistrust anybody under fifty, useless engineers who cannot imagine anything beyond their calculating ruler, "experienced" architects who feel they do not need to learn anything any more, people with a hierarchical chip in their brain... Unfortunately, one has to put up with some of this crap because sometimes the system does not recognise even the most obvious things, like for example that the people who are actually doing the jobs in every single office are under forty, and mostly even under thirty. And they are the only ones able to do the job because they can use computers, because they have access to technical means that have become central to the production processes. And because they work as a research process, producing knowledge as they are producing the project, rather than accumulating "experience".

With Yokohama, our managers said that we would need between 30 and 40 architects working on the job. We are managing with 14. If we had followed their advice, not only we would have gone bankrupt, we would have sacrificed the project's sophistication, as the energy that now is concentrated in a few good people would have been lost in meetings, timesheets, minutes, and other things invented by managers to justify their incapacity to produce, and their privileges in the hierarchy. It was perhaps our academic experience that reassured us of the value of keeping a team structure that also produces knowledge, rather than just drawings. One of the things you learn from teaching is that there are virtually no limits to the capacity of people to produce — knowledge and stuff — as long as they remain motivated. It is only experience that teaches us where our limits are, and once we have learned that, we are finished, because our work can be calculated and measured, becomes stratified and ceases to be a weapon. It was also our academic background that allowed us to put together a dream-team of architects whose individual skills and commitment went beyond conventional measure, and whose presence could have specific impact on the work. Like in a good band.

Despite the constant requirement of our client for a clear hierarchy of command, we structured the work around the production of packages, giving independence to the designers to research, develop and produce the drawings for each package: partitions, glazing, ceiling, traffic, structure, mechanical services... We tried to avoid any centralisation of command, as the team was sufficiently small and close to allow us to rely on everybody to keep track of all fronts of development: individual platoons. Have a war at work. Anything to avoid stratification, professionalisation. Everybody goes to meetings, makes copies, meets contractors, makes coffee, talks to consultants, fixes computers, does accounts... Of course it has come at a price: no 9 to 5, no holidays, no weekends... This experiment is about pushing things to the limit, occupying everybody's life with the project for as long as it lasts and is interesting. The process is aimed at reaching maximum intensity, suspending all limitations of work and projecting it as far as possible.

The structural development of the project — carried out together with SDG — has become the main source of ideas for its implementation, and a trail of discovery that reaches far beyond the images that have become the better known side of the project. The structure that we proposed in the competition was made out of a folded piece of steel, as an attempt to make the structure consistent with the general concept of the project as a folded organisation. This proposal was also advantageous in terms of its resistance to earthquake stresses and akin to the techniques of the naval industry to which the building was affiliated. The "cardboard" structure emerged out of what was originally a reference to the local tradition of "origami" construction. These references to local construction systems, both literal and culturally mediated, were an attempt to contextualise the proposal without having to resort to the mimicry of local building. In other words, the context was introduced as a process of material organisation, rather than as an image. This sensitivity to the local will have a decisive role in the generation of the building's geometry, through the extraordinary importance that the latent asymmetry of the grounding conditions on site will play during the design development phase.

At the beginning of the design development, the structure was clearly the most critical point of the project, as the competition scheme proposal was as interesting as it was naïve, and needed substantial technical development to become realisable without betraying the original purpose. The main problem was how to solve a three-dimensionally complex geometry with a geometry that was basically axial – that of folding. The outcome of the process so far has been interesting, as it has originated important geometrical and formal emergences directly out of the pragmatics of the project, rather than as a kind of external formal or geometrical ideology imposed on the project from the outside.

During the development of the basic design phase, we came up with a solution where the folds of the web were being woven with each other every half fold, so that we could achieve the curvature at a larger scale. This is a structural geometry that has been used, for example, by Nervi, Piano and others to make large-span shells with a kind of structural unit or cell that is repeated along curves. But what was interesting is that the cells of the structure would become differentiated at every point of the surface, much like in an organic system. One of the immediate implications of this system is that we removed the lower plate of the structure to simplify the construction, turning the folded metal plates into a crucial expressive trait of the project: the origami had finally become visible.

continues on page 33

The interdisciplinarity you're pursuing in *Verb*, as in any project, is interesting. As you know, I've always been in favour of it. But perhaps for me it's more a matter of quality than of concept. Perhaps a matter of craft and, ultimately, discipline, although inevitably the construction of space is a multidisciplinary task. The multidisciplinary world has made a lot of mistakes over the last ten years, simply because the people who claim to know how to produce with computers tend to have very superficial knowledge, either of the specific discipline of production or of computers themselves. The dangerous thing about computers is that, whether you know your way around something or not, whether or not you have ideas, you press a key and something happens anyway. After insisting for ten years on multidisciplinary forms of production, and on the computer as a production tool, I believe that ultimately you also need the context of the specific profession or discipline to be able to direct and adjust production efficiently. And in our case, the discipline is architecture. No matter what routes we use to produce something, we nevertheless need that reference framework to move forward.

DEVELOPMENT OF THE STRUCTURAL DESIGN *KUNIO WATANABE*

President,
Structural Design Group (SDG)

STRUCTURE OF THE ORIGINAL SCHEME

At the time the competition was held we were in the middle of the construction of Tokyo International Forum, and were preoccupied with the site supervision work on that project. Although we knew that a competition expressing the international ambitions of Yokohama was being held, we regarded it as something occurring in another world with no relation to us, and therefore showed no interest.

In May 1995 the results were widely publicized in the architectural press and I heard that the FOA scheme had been selected as the overall winner. I still clearly remember the impact that the scheme had. The structural concept in the FOA scheme used no beams or columns. "A folding floor structure changes into the next floor, and also forms the mechanism to transfer stresses". It was a structure found nowhere in the world, a structural approach both innovative and without precedent. They called this floor system "cardboard structure" and presented it using the axonometric shown below.

I had the vague feeling that the technological expertise, which we had built up through our work over the years, would enable us to help realize this strange structure. A year of negotiations followed from the autumn of that year until autumn the next year, when SDG were finally appointed as structural engineer for the project. These negotiations were managed by our staff member at that time Alan Burden (now Associate Professor, Kanto Gakuin University). The profuse telephone, fax and mail records of these negotiations were filed as the conversations between Alan, Alejandro Zaero-Polo and Farshid Moussavi developed. Even today it is interesting to read these records. In order to progress the project, FOA were negotiating with Yokohama City, convincing related parties, and planning the appointment of various consultants. In particular, regarding the structure, they were in a position where they had to handle their relationship with the Ove Arup in London very carefully. It was perhaps a time when all their energies were exhausted in establishing a design environment rather than in working to improve the content of the architectural scheme.

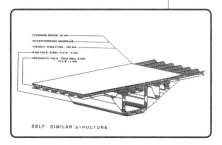

SELF-SIMILAR STRUCTURE.

The present trusting relationship between FOA and SDG was built on the sincere will contained in the communications four years ago between Alan and FOA. It is clear that without the competition and the "cardboard" concept the two design teams would never have met.

INITIAL SCHEME

When we first made a technical appraisal of the "cardboard" structure we could not agree with its rationality. Since our job is not about how faithfully we can follow an initial scheme, but rather about how an initial scheme can best be developed, we made central to our design work an analysis of this "continuously folded floor structure" from the most general standpoint, searching amongst the widest set of structural factors for those which were actually possible. Stated broadly, the areas for structural study fixed in December 1996 covered ten items.

1. POSSIBILITIES FOR THE STRUCTURAL SYSTEM

SUPERSTRUCTURE. Consideration of a two-skin system in steel plate with the upper and lower surfaces transferring tension, compression and shear force.

A   structural effectiveness
B   resistance of steel plate to buckling
C   ease of fabrication
D   economy of steel plate
E   market conditions

These and other factors were considered for the case of a basic steel plate thickness of 9mm. In order to control stresses and deflections a maximum plate thickness of 25mm was permitted. In consideration of weldability of the plate grade SM490 was the preferred material.

The depth of the two-skin deck was varied according to the required structural performance. A basic dimension of 600mm was used, varying between a minimum of 250mm and a maximum of 3000mm. For transfer of out-of-plane shear stresses, three configurations were considered depending on the depth of the deck; a full web system when the deck was of the order of 600mm, a honeycomb web where service runs were required, and an open lattice where the depth exceeded 900mm.

In order to transfer forces through the deck, consideration was given to the use of shell action in such a way that a good balance would be achieved between membrane stresses and out-of-plane bending stresses.

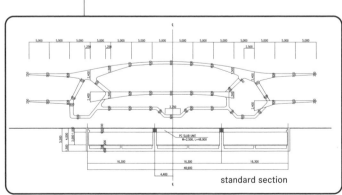

standard section

Research was carried out into methods of support. The number of supports in the initial scheme was insufficient.

The external facades would be cantilevered, with no supports along the perimeter.

The durability of the inside of the deck needed to be improved.

Consideration was needed into maintenance systems.

Consideration of overall durability was needed.

Glass or non-corrosive aluminium would be used for exterior sculptures and cladding panels.

Mullions used within the glazing plane would be connected vertically to floor planes above and below, so that they could act not only to resist wind load, but also to help control deflections and vibrations.

SUBSTRUCTURE. At apron level a large span (48m) slab in prestressed concrete would be used.

Intermediate supporting columns would also be in prestressed concrete, connected to the apron level slab using high-tensile rods. parboos

Attention was given to the water-tightness of the foundation mat slab and retaining walls.

OVERALL STRUCTURE. No expansion joints would be used within the structure.

2. DEFINITION OF GEOMETRY

Defining factors

A   system for definition of coordinates
B   exploitation of membrane stresses
C   rules for fabrication
D   rules for assembly
E   integration with finishes and services routes

The necessity or otherwise for structural coordinates to be parallel with finishes coordinates.

The need or otherwise for an adjustable geometry

The need or otherwise for the geometries of the upper and lower surfaces to be the same.

The use of an orthogonal grid or a segmental grid centered on a sphere.

Forms for investigation:

A   flat plane
B   cylinder
C   sloped spherical surface
D   conical surface
E   rotated parabola
F   rotated doubly-curved surface
G   surface of rotation based on a triangular function
H   a combination of several surfaces

3. STRUCTURAL UNIT

Whether the definition of structural unit and fabrication unit are actually separate problems or not.

The feasibility of a unit system.

Consideration of a basic 70m-wide unit.

4. JOINT SYSTEM

Various welding types

Friction-grip bolts

Feasibility of dry joints

Joints in the surface

System for joints at the intersection between deck plates

System for joints at the lower supports

5. ANALYSIS MODELS

Static 3-D analysis model

Dynamic 3-D analysis model

Vibrational modelling of the interaction between supporting ground, piles and building

Definition of section sizes

6. DEFLECTIONS AND STRESSES DUE TO VERTICAL, EARTHQUAKE, WIND AND TEMPERATURE

Estimation of floor loads, floor surfacing, waterproofing, ceiling construction, services specification, corrosion protection and fireproofing for the terminal and the plaza.

Research required into appropriate imposed loads during earthquake.

Establishment of earthquake waves and input energy, and preliminary analysis.

Planning of wind-tunnel testing, preliminary analysis of expected wind pressures, weighting of wind directions.

Establishment of design temperature variations – day and night, summer and winter, members subject to direct sunlight.

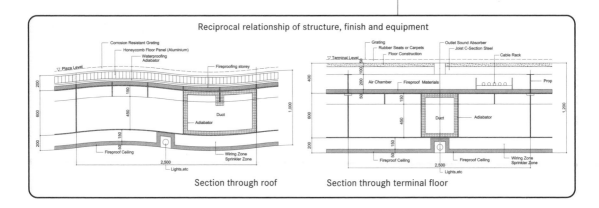

Reciprocal relationship of structure, finish and equipment

Section through roof   Section through terminal floor

7. FOUNDATION STRUCTURE AND PLANNING OF PILING WORKS

Comparative study of capacity, construct ability and economy of various types of pile. Fixing of foundation type.

Since the ground is susceptible to liquefaction under seismic action a wide-ranging study into this aspect was required.

Investigation into the possibility of negative skin friction on piles, and future foundation settlement.

Overall comparison of pile performance

1   hollow PC under-reamed piles.
2   pre-bored hollow PC under-reamed piles
3   steel pipe piles
4   cast-in-place concrete piles
5   cast-in-place under-reamed piles

8. CONSTRUCTION PLANNING, FABRICATION, TRANSPORTATION, ERECTION

If transportation were to be by sea using barges cranes would be required for loading and unloading. If transported by sea while suspended, the process would be affected by weather conditions and three 3000 tonne cranes would be needed.

Feasibility of laying rails along the site and transporting by side-sliding erection.

Fabrication of 70m wide units based on lateral cuts.

Both the fabrication unit and the erection method would differ depending on whether the units were a three-level integrated piece or a section where the floor was separated at each level. Consideration into sliding the sections, which act as support pieces into position and then inserting intermediate sections.

Investigation into feasibility of erecting the structure without encroaching on a 15m strip down one side.

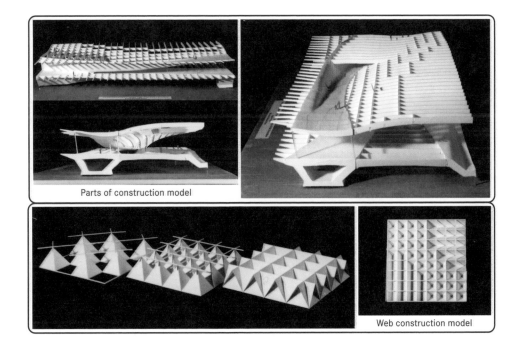

Parts of construction model

Web construction model

9. CONSTRUCTION COST (STRUCTURAL COST)

Estimation of quantity of steel in superstructure and cost of substructure.

Improvement in accuracy of estimation as design was developed.

For steelwork the costs of materials, fabrication, transportation, and erection were separated.

Assessment of common and direct temporary works costs.

Assessment of temporary frames required for transportation and erection, and of heavy equipment.

10. CONSTRUCTION SCHEDULE

Construction sequence

Environmental considerations

Fixing construction conditions

Preparation of construction schedule

Overall assessment of design and construction based on overall timing of construction

Based on an investigation of these ten areas, our initial proposed scheme was the space-frame shown in the figures below.

This scheme used the smallest amount of steel and had good construct ability, it was structurally rational, and arrived at through giving weight to practical considerations in the construction.

DEVELOPMENT OF 3-D STRUCTURAL SCHEME BASED AROUND THE "CARDBOARD" CONCEPT

Our method of structural planning is not one, which proceeds linearly. Rather it has characteristics whereby our thinking develops over plane. In the original 1997 scheme too much emphasis was placed on producing a practicable scheme. Reflecting on the fact that the structural concept implicit in FOA's competition scheme had not been exploited properly, we set about re-appraising the design at the start of 1998.

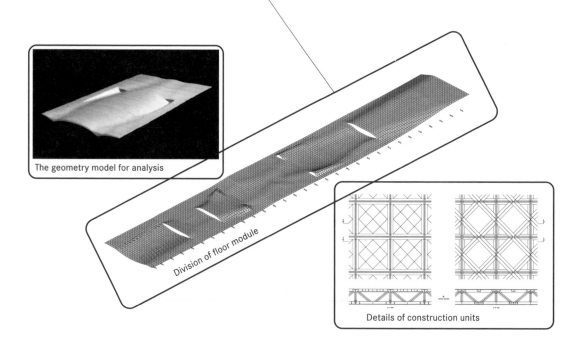

The geometry model for analysis

Division of floor module

Details of construction units

The axonometric below shows a very small part of the floor model for the structure. It can be easily understood from the arrows on the diagrams, which show the size and direction of force from the analysis, that the stresses in each part of the folded floor are steadily attracted into the slope.

This analysis models the floor as a single plate, recognizing that one area of the floor structure changes into the next.

Regarding the composition of the "basic unit" for this continuous floor, we re-thought the problem taking the "cardboard structure" concept of the competition scheme as our starting point.

Figure 1 on the following page shows the "cardboard" of the competition scheme. This structure cannot transmit forces in two directions. At the intersection between the flange and web plates there is no problem in transmitting forces in the X-direction – but in the Y-direction an eccentricity "e" arises.

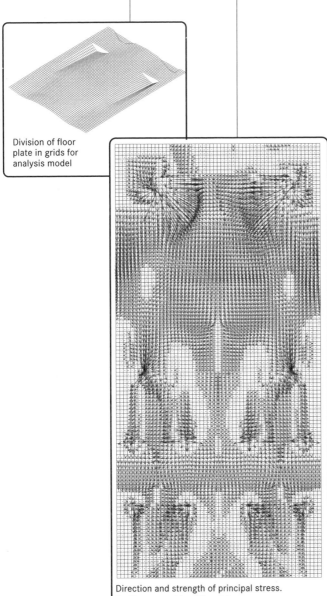

Division of floor
plate in grids for
analysis model

…and the lower side of the plate.

Direction and strength of principal stress.
On the upper side of the plate…

Because of the moments generated by this eccentricity it becomes necessary to use thick plates for the flange. In fact the flange plate needs to be about 30mm thick and is therefore uneconomic.

If it is attempted to absorb these local moments in the web, then the section becomes that shown in figure 2, and more steel is used in the web structure than the flange, which is supposed to be the main member.

In order to eliminate this wastage it is necessary to align the axes of flange and web as shown in figure 3, which raises the question of whether it is possible to join on a line. Even if it is possible to fabricate the line joint, the contradiction remains that in the X-direction there is a full web, whilst in the Y-direction the web is of a lattice form. In order to distribute forces in three dimensions an orthotropic section was desirable.

A section, which is orthotropic and has good resistance to buckling, is one similar to that shown in figure 4. The web members are grouped together to give an arrangement close to pin-jointed, making the connection to the flange plate very difficult.

Therefore, if the flange is made not from a plate, but from discrete elements, its relationship with the web becomes easier, and orthotropic performance can be maintained in figure 5. This is the main reason for pursuing the "spaceframe structure" which forms the basis of the initial scheme. It can also be considered as the method, which covers the largest area with the smallest amount of steel.

Starting from FOA's "cardboard" scheme, if the web is arranged as a grillage as shown in figure 6, the orthotropic behaviour and ease of construction can be maintained. In this case unless webs are provided at a close pitch the flange plate buckles, and considerable steel plate is required as reinforcement, taking away the rationality of the scheme.

This demerit can be eliminated by the use of a honeycomb arrangement of the web as shown in figure 7. Several examples of structures using such systems do exist, but generally there is a need for the

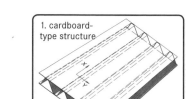

1. cardboard-type structure

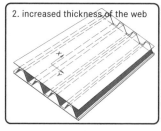

2. increased thickness of the web

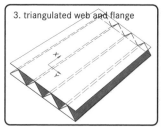

3. triangulated web and flange

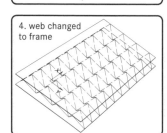

4. web changed to frame

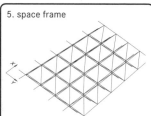

5. space frame

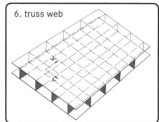

6. truss web

development of special welding techniques to achieve a connection between the flange and the honeycomb, which can transmit large forces.

Instead of considering "How to make the welds?" we noticed that an effective solution was also possible by cutting out Styrofoam in the form of figure 8 and attaching steel plate to both faces using adhesive. There already exist many examples of such construction in timber structures. If there is an effective adhesive and sufficient sectional properties in the Styrofoam, then a lightweight flange will not buckle, and it is possible to make a freely curved shape. In this case it would be necessary to develop a new adhesive, which is both strong and heat-resistant.

If it were decided not to rely on such an adhesive, then it would also be possible to carry the forces between flange and a cast web by bond forces. Figure 9 shows a scheme with shear connectors attached to the flange plate and the internal void filled with aerated concrete. It is possible to achieve a specific gravity of 0.6 with current aerated concrete, and if designed properly this may also allow the elimination of fire-protection. Service runs may also be cast-in if they are fitted in position beforehand.

Collecting these ideas, placing the "cardboard structure" idea at the center of figure 10, the axis to the right moves toward a spaceframe, a scheme based on pursuing lightness through the use of VOIDS, whereas the axis to the left uses an infill material to achieve a SOLID structure.

The VOID direction places the pursuit of lightness through modern structural technology above all else, and is the same as the initial scheme. The SOLID direction on the other hand follows a rational axis to mix various materials and move from simple steelwork to a hybrid structure, a type that has not as yet been adequately explored in the field of structures.

Further, from a structural point of view, the VOID direction is suited to structures where tension is dominant, while the SOLID direction suits structures where compression dominates.

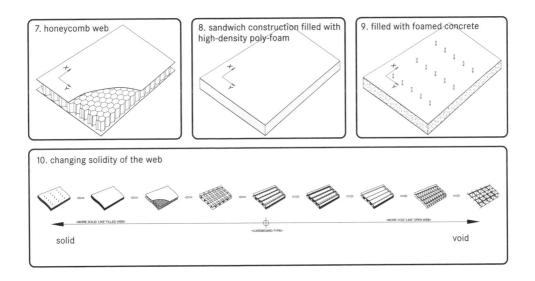

7. honeycomb web

8. sandwich construction filled with high-density poly-foam

9. filled with foamed concrete

10. changing solidity of the web

<MORE SOLID 'LIKE' FILLED WEB>   <CARDBOARD-TYPE>   <MORE VOID 'LIKE' OPEN WEB>

solid   void

Through the use of some form of infill material the problem of buckling of the thin steel plate is solved at a basic level, and if this material has even a small compressive strength, it can improve the compression resistance of the whole above that which could be achieved through a normal flange and web structural arrangement.

Based on these ideas an improved scheme was developed. This scheme uses plates of approximately 6mm thickness for the upper and lower flanges. In order to form the smoothly curved surfaces required, the plate is folded based on a triangular pattern with a 2.5m grid. Four materials are used for the web structure joining the flanges. The first is of vierendeel form joining the plates orthogonally. The second are lattice members. The third is a full-web steel plate, and the last cast infill concrete. The four forms of web are employed in positions appropriate to the distribution of stresses within the structure.

In this way the continuously curved surfaces can be fully structured, and a structure without columns or beams is realized.

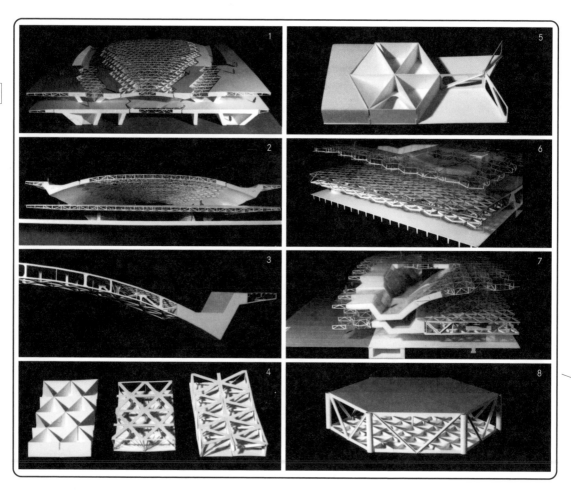

TOWARDS A LINEAR STRUCTURE, AWAY FROM A 3D STRUCTURE.

The greatest merit of the improved scheme is that forces are transferred naturally within the 3D surface enabling an effortless, light structure. At the same time, the greatest de-merit is the poor construct ability of the scheme. With this form of 3-D structure, stability is not achieved until all erection work is complete. During construction temporary support is required at almost every location, imposing limits on how much the construction period can be reduced.

In February 1999 a fax arrived at SDG from Alejandro Zaera-Polo. We had exchanged faxes extensively up until that point, but the fax of that day left a particularly deep impression, so that I still remember it well. His suggestion was that while the possibilities of the structure extending in 3D were good, he wanted to re-assess the possibilities of a scheme closer to that of the competition where the two lines of ramps acted as main girders and arch members spanned between them, with cantilevers extending off from the outer side of these girders. A suitable structure would be a folded plate, with the upper steel plate left as the surface, and the lower plate omitted to expose the underside in the interior space. I found the suggestion very appealing.

The form was now one where the undulating surface was no longer continuously changing to be absorbed in the ramps in a 3D manner, but one based on a concept different from that so far explored. It starts from the idea that if the structure is linear it should be possible to use a structure based around ring cuts along the long axis of the structure. From the proportions of the facility (width 70m, length 420m), the feasibility appeared good. At that point the previous schemes were put aside, and we started work on a full appraisal of Zaera-Polo's proposal, to arrive at the current scheme.

I had been too preoccupied with the concept of a "continuously undulating floor". Once we started to think about a gradually changing ring cut structure the problems with the scheme until then were steadily solved. In retrospect it appears the obvious solution, but this was the major leap towards realization.

See page 36   See page 38

1 development of a model
  with greater opening of
  the web
2 interior of the open-web
  model
3 web construction
  model
4 units of triangular grids
5 units of hexagonal grids
6 relationship between
  construction and
  equipment units
7 hexagonal web
  structure
8 construction detail of
  hexagonal units

COMBINATION OF GIRDERS AND FOLDED PLATE STRUCTURE

The two lines of box girders change shape while undulating both in plan and 3D. These steel girders serve as the spine of this building functionally, mechanically, and structurally. Within the girders stiffeners are located appropriately to prevent buckling, but in the region of the supports where compressive forces are high, sections are also infilled with concrete to produce a hybrid structure.

Within the folded steel plate structure large forces are developed at the apex of each triangle, and suitable flanges are provided. For the sloping surfaces thin plates are used. Since it is not possible to weld the thin plates, the junction with flanges is made using rivet-type joints. For the connection between the folded plates and the girder also, a mechanical rather than welded connection has been proposed in the current scheme.

If work now enters detailed design, and construction begins, then further development of the scheme will occur. Through completion of this building we are looking forward to further deepening our relationship with FOA. We have also asked for the opportunity to report on the structural design two years hence once the facility is completed.

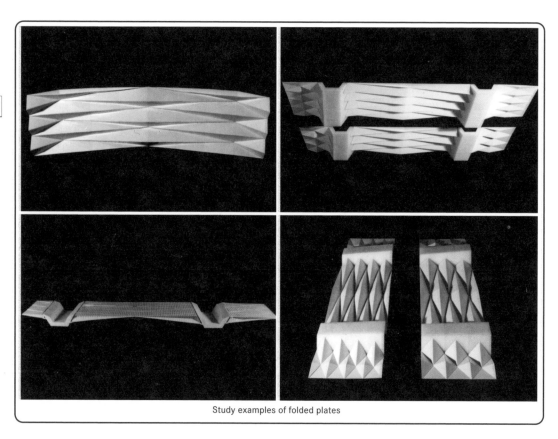

Study examples of folded plates

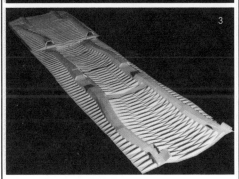

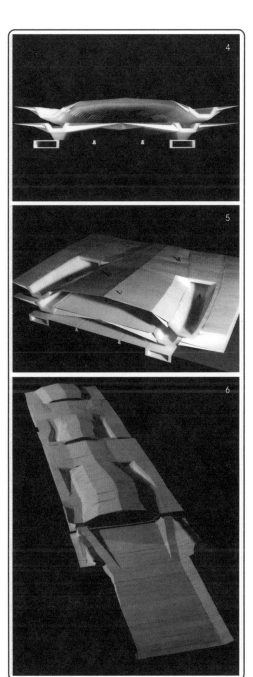

1,2 study examples of folded plates
3 second model generation (ceiling)
4 first model generation
5 first model generation
6 second model generation

we pick up here on the text by Alejandro Zaera-Polo
interrupted on page 18.

During the development of the basic design phase, we came up with a solution where the folds of the web were being woven with each other every half fold, so that we could achieve the curvature at a larger scale. This is a structural geometry that has been used, for example, by Nervi, Piano and others to make large-span shells with a kind of structural unit or cell that is repeated along curves. But what was interesting is that the cells of the structure would become differentiated at every point of the surface, much like in an organic system. One of the immediate implications of this system is that we removed the lower plate of the structure to simplify the construction, turning the folded metal plates into a crucial expressive trait of the project: the origami had finally become visible.

At this point there was an interesting debate on whether the structural system had to become a kind of isotropic shell with local singularities, as the computer perspectives seemed to indicate, or whether it should retain the bi-directional qualities that the plan of the building contained, becoming a system composed by two series of large-scale folds bridged by a series of transversal folds. After testing a kind of hybrid between the original "cardboard" type and a kind of space frame with local densification, we realised that the concentration of axial stresses along the longitudinal large-scale folds suggested that the structural type had to be altered to become a concrete-filled structure. This was why we decided that, despite the image of the building, the bi-directional structure was finally a more suitable structural solution. The coincidence between the ramp system and the main longitudinal girders became the primary determinant of the structural geometry, as the conflict between the symmetrical condition of the programmatic structure and the asymmetrical condition of the grounding system forced us to bend the ramps. The edges of the building were located 15m from the pier's edges to comply with the symmetrical location of the boarding decks on both sides, while the foundations could only reach up to 21.5m from the Shinko side and 29m on the Yamashita side. This conflict between structural asymmetry and programmatic symmetry was already present in the competition entry, but had not been fully exploited, as it had been absorbed entirely in the lower level ramps, without affecting the geometry of the upper level. It was only when we had to start thinking about the correlation between the two levels of girders that the asymmetry extended through the whole geometry, rather than being confined to the lower level. One of the criticisms we received after the competition scheme was made public was that the topology of the building was basically symmetrical and Beaux-Arts. However, it was

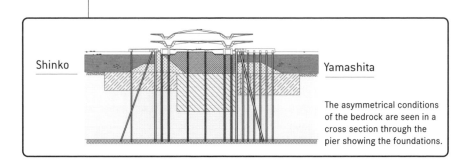

Shinko

Yamashita

The asymmetrical conditions of the bedrock are seen in a cross section through the pier showing the foundations.

Process of increase in the resolution of the cross sections (see text on page 37)

not that we did not consider this problem during the competition stage, but rather that we thought it was more interesting to preserve the conflict as a generative trigger than to impose a formal ideology – asymmetry – on the problem. Sensitivity to the initial conditions of the brief and reference to the local shipbuilding industry had become productive in the process of formal determination.

The other subject evolving through the development of the project has been the determination of the grid, the geometrical fabric of the project. At the competition stage, our proposal was generated by analysing the spatial locations of the different spaces of the terminal, such as the boarding decks, visitors' decks, rooftop plaza, departure and arrival hall, and traffic plaza, and link them locally through a deformed surface. This surface was constructed through a sequence of parallel transversal sections, describing the local conditions every 15m, and morphing them along the axis of the building. The interesting question arising from the process of evolution of the grid was its ambiguity between an organisational technique based on parallel bands and the single-surface technique that absorbs differences into singularities of a congruent space. We were interested basically in the single-surface effect, but our methods were still reliant on the techniques that we had learned at OMA, where the sequences of parallel bands developed from La Villette through The Hague City Hall and the Grande Bibliothèque produced organisations that allowed for a maximum sectional flexibility: a kind of rotated "plan libre" aimed at reaching maximum programmatic freedom across levels.

In so doing, though, our programmatic aims – the coherence of the circulation diagram across programs – were radically different from the programmatic incongruence and juxtaposition that originated OMA's infamous band technique. The predominant longitudinal direction of the building and the basically symmetrical programmatic structure supported the use of this organisation, producing a conflict with our interest in programmatic continuity that will drive the evolution of the project through detail design. The conflict between a striated organisation and a smooth congruence that we had seen also between the grounding conditions and the programmatic symmetry was also present in this inadequacy between ambitions and technique of organisation. A key point to stress is that despite its "in-formal" appearance, our ambition for this project – and most other ones – is of a radical formal determination. The informal appearance for us is nothing but the outcome of processes of highly complex formal determination. This is the aim of integrative addition as the form of organisation of the process...

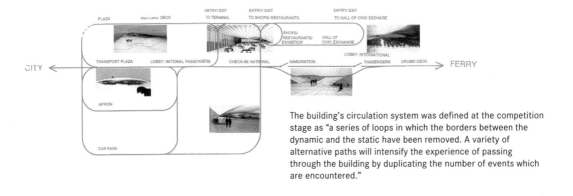

The building's circulation system was defined at the competition stage as "a series of loops in which the borders between the dynamic and the static have been removed. A variety of alternative paths will intensify the experience of passing through the building by duplicating the number of events which are encountered."

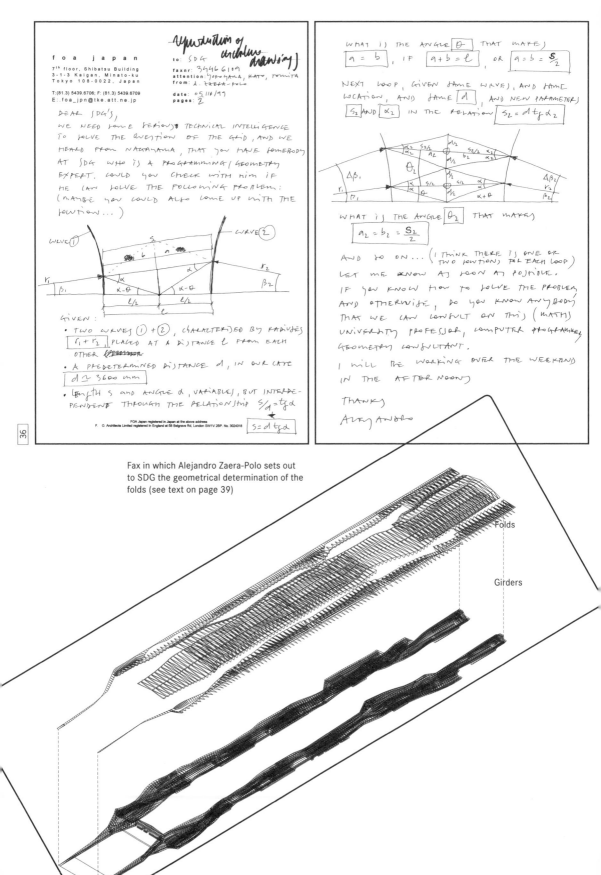

Fax in which Alejandro Zaera-Polo sets out to SDG the geometrical determination of the folds (see text on page 39)

In this process of constant increase in the determination of the geometry of the project, our first step was to increase the resolution of the transversal sections from 15m to 5m, by inserting two new sections within each band. The technique we used to determine the new intermediate sections was achieved by producing what we called "control lines" or curves that were determined by the points of location of each element in the transversal sections – boarding and visitors' decks, parking, halls, etc. – turned into spline curves. This was the first technique in which we started to establish an argument of consistency between the different sections, produced out of the determinations of successive local conditions. By cutting the "control lines" through intermediate planes, we were able to locate the position of the different elements longitudinally. At the same time, we dropped the originally splined geometry of the surface into a geometry of complex curves made out of a palette of 7 radiuses, producing the surface out of the intersection of cylindrical or conical surfaces of regular radiuses, in order to simplify the manufacturing process. This process produced 96 transversal sections to determine the form of the building that were clearly insufficient for a detailed description of the project. So, due also to a change in the basic size of the transversal folds, we increased the resolution to a grid of 3.6m, still using the "control curves" as our technique of coherence. Soon, the 124 transversal sections we obtained doubled, as the basic scale of the transversal folds was fixed to 1.8m, which became the new resolution of the grid. The process of geometrical development became basically a problem of increasing the resolution of the grid, and every step in this process required an exponential increase in the amount of information we had to produce. When we started the detailed design of the girder's geometry, we realised that even this amount of information was not sufficient to control precisely the geometry of the project. We also noticed that by rolling parallel sections along curved control lines we were producing irregularities in the geometry of the ramps, unless we differentiated between the transversal sections of the girders. Even worse: because of the existing geometrical definition, every face of the girder would have to be triangulated, and different from each other, and every transversal fold had become a different geometry. Even if now we had control of the determination of the stiffeners that constructed the girders, we had no control over the triangulation of their faces.

One of the most important evolutions in the project occurred at this point, when we started to consider the construction of the girders through the rotation of the same stiffener templates at regular

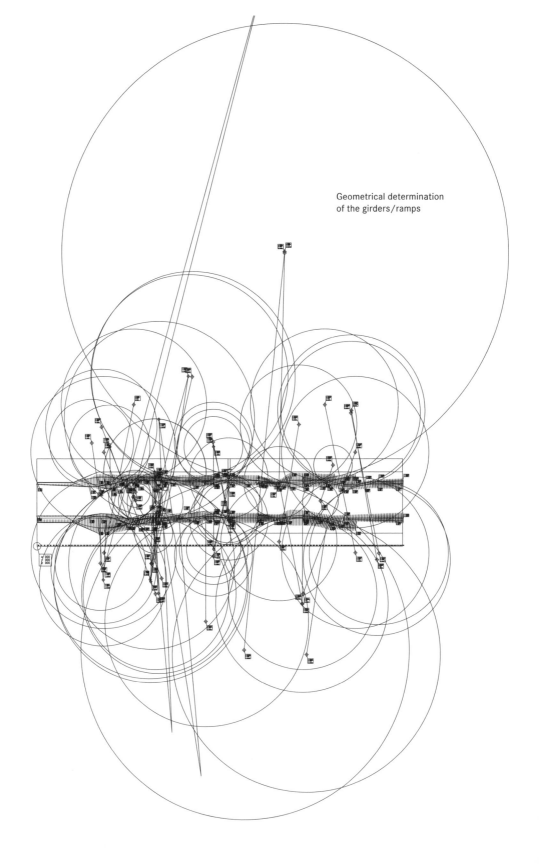

Geometrical determination
of the girders/ramps

intervals along the "control lines", that also now had to be dropped into complex curves. In order to increase the regularity of the manufacturing process, we started, simultaneously, to consider the possibility of producing local symmetry in the transversal folds, by making them meet the girders at a perpendicular angle. The only way to achieve this, given the deformed geometry of the girders, was to shift from the parallel transversal grid of the competition entry, to a topological grid originating in the control lines that determined the girders' geometry. In our new topological grid, the parallel bands did not grant independence to the different parts, but on the contrary, it established functions that connected them to each other, considerably diminishing the amount of information required for the determination of the form. We had therefore moved from a "raster" space, where each point is determined by local information, to a vector space, where each point is determined by differentiated global orders. Again, there was no ideological or critical statement in making this step, but rather the pragmatic solution of technical conflicts in the process of development. We feel that it is this kind of discovery that can turn processes of a purely technical nature into architectural discipline, to let the discipline emerge from the production rather than from a critical or ideological relation to the previous constitution of the discipline.

The next conflict emerged between the possibility of achieving repetition in the girder's geometry or symmetry in the transversal folds. As the folds will have to link with the girders at the stiffener locations, if we wanted local symmetry of the folds, we would have to sacrifice regularity in the girders' sections, as the pitch of the stiffeners will be determined by the intersection of the folds with the girder's edge. If, conversely, we started with a regular pitch of the stiffeners in the girders, we would have to sacrifice the local symmetry of the folds. In order to set up a non-parallel grid to solve the problem, we first gave priority to the local symmetry of the folds, to determine the position of the stiffeners along the girders. The position of the new gridlines was not geometrically determined, and had to be calculated numerically through a program that established iteration loops to calculate the intersection of the transversal folds' local axis with the curved edges of the girders. As a program, the iteration loops had to be calculated sequentially, so its results would depend on the area of the plan where we started calculating the iteration loops.

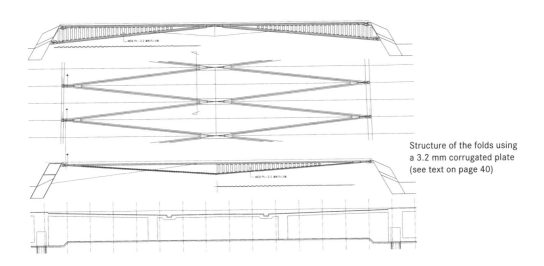

Structure of the folds using a 3.2 mm corrugated plate (see text on page 40)

However, due to the fact that after calculation, over 65% of the steel weight was concentrated on the girders, we decided to take a grid determined by rolling templates along the "control lines" at regular intervals, so that the girder's construction would become as regular as possible. In this option, the fabric of the folds had to become anti-symmetrical in the central folds – still identical in terms of formal determination – and symmetrical in the lateral folds, leaving only the two intermediate folds of every arch to be irregular. A third scale of folding will be produced at this stage in the process: in order to reduce the total weight of steel, we had to place small stiffeners inside the small-scale transversal folds that were resulting in great increases in the manufacturing costs. In order to avoid this increase we decided to replace the 6mm thick plates, that constituted the first proposal for the detail of the folds, with a 3.2mm corrugated plate. The corrugations will provide the plates with enough strength to avoid the stiffeners.

The process is not yet finished, although most of the crucial decisions have already been made. In one of the recent meetings with the contractors to explain the geometry of the project and the process of setting out on site, they were asking us for the co-ordinates of the points of the building, as if the form was decided a priori, and they needed just to implement that geometry on site. To their surprise, we had to explain to them that the geometry was strictly related to the manufacturing and construction systems, and could be modified if necessary. They said that they had thought that site control was going to be the most crucial aspect in the construction process, but now they realised that the most important process was to be the manufacturing. One of them pointed out that they would have to use the same techniques used to build rollercoasters, where the setting out utilises local references between identical templates rolled along irregular three-dimensional geometry. Exactly! – as we said – Rollercoaster construction!

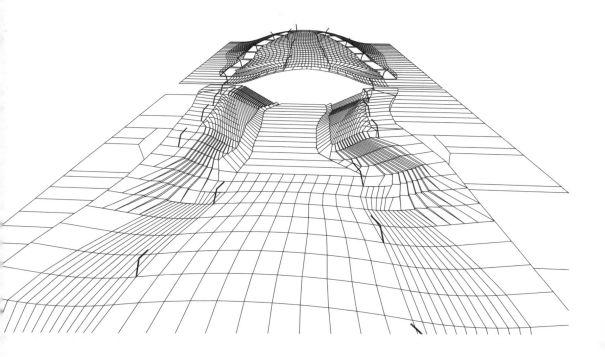

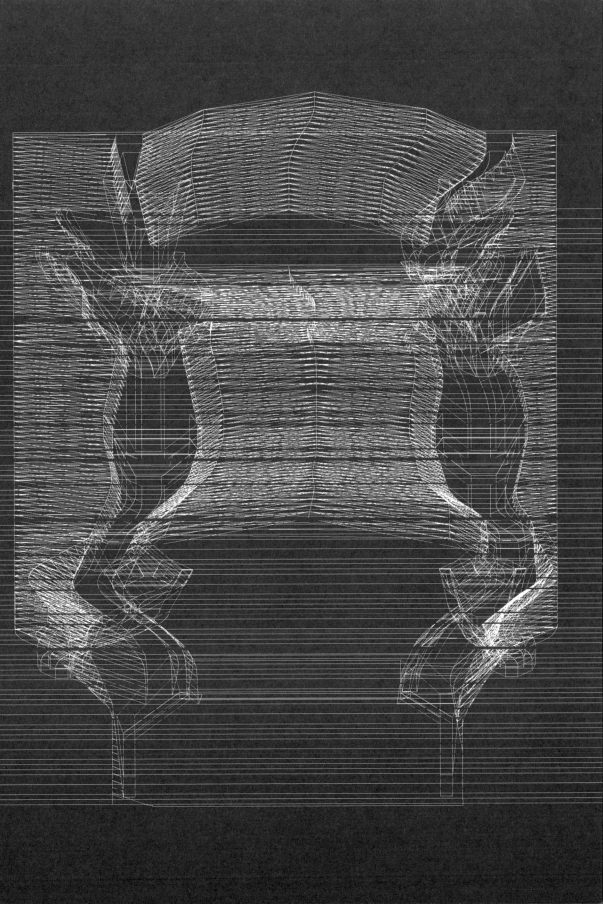

Generation of the lower and upper ramps

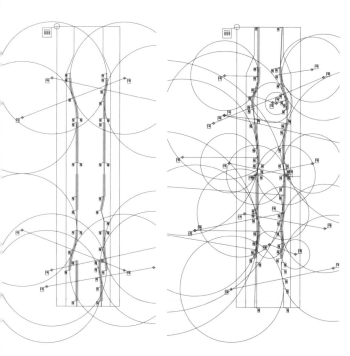

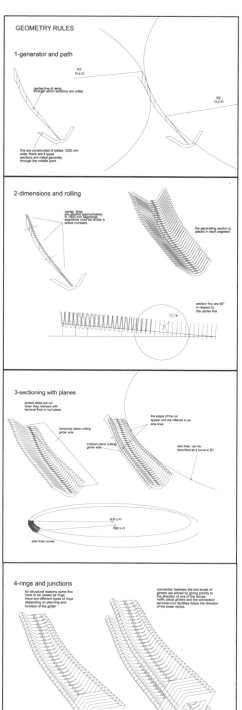

GEOMETRY RULES

1-generator and path

R1
(x,y,z)

center line of ramp
through which sections are rolled

R2
(x,y,z)

fins are constructed of plates 1200 mm
wide; there are 4 types
sections are rolled generally
through the middle point

2-dimensions and rolling

center lines
are divided approximately
in 1800 mm segments,
segments must be divide in
whole numbers

the generating section is
placed in each segment

90°

section fins are 90°
in respect to
the center line

3-sectioning with planes

girders sides are cut
when they intersect with
terminal floor or roof plaza

horizontal plane cutting
girder side

the edges of the cut
appear and are referred to as
side lines

inclined plane cutting
girder side

side lines can be
described as a curve in 3D

R1(x,y,z)

R2(x,y,z)

side lines curves

4-rings and junctions

for structural reasons some fins
have to be closed as rings
there are different types of rings
depending on planning and
function of the girder

connection between the two levels of
girders are solved by giving priority to
the direction of one of the ramps;
traffic plaza girders and the connection
terminal-civic facilities follow the direction
of the lower ramps

ring

connection

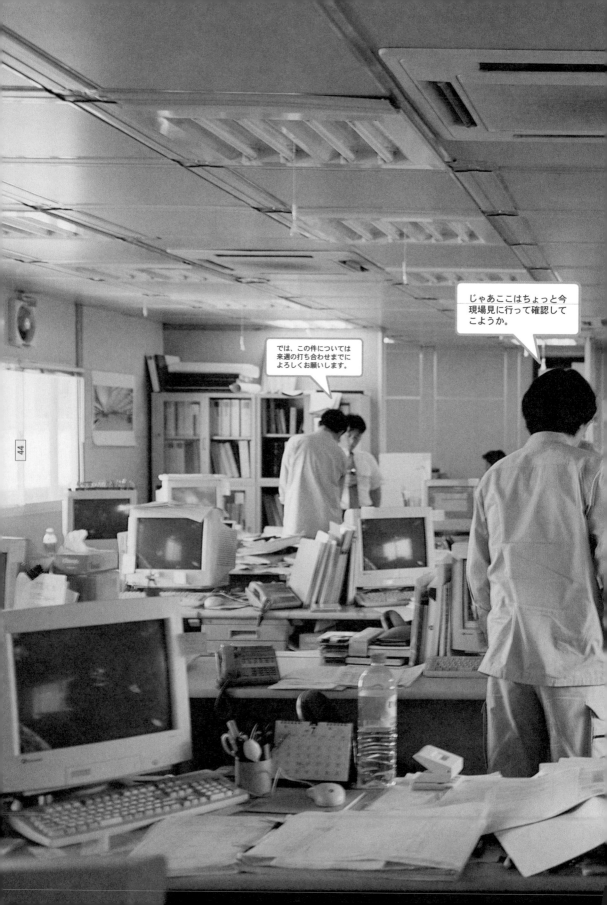

FARSHID MOUSSAVI >

The project has been changing constantly, and I have always thought that it would be great to find a venue to show the way we have been incorporating these changes. We talk of the 'add-in' rather than 'add-on' process – every new information entering the project at any stage has been given the possibility to shape the project directly. The 'plan' at any time is therefore simply the state that it is, given the level of intelligence it has reached. We talk about the building as a fish that constantly moves. It is funny even for us to look back at the earlier plans as they are so different to the latest ones that we are working on. The terminal plan shows the changes most. As you were particularly interested in process, I thought you may want to see the evolution of this plan. I got excited about this 'history of the terminal' and I have been opening each file, cleaning up, removing texts, etc. and compiling them next to each other in order. (turn to next page)

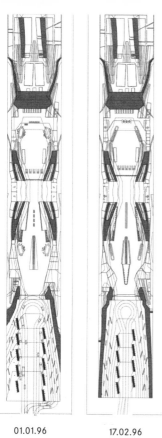
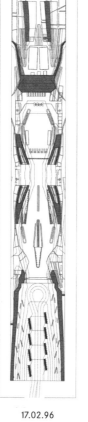
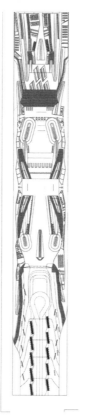
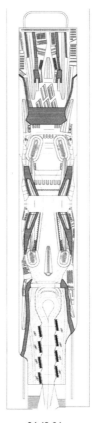
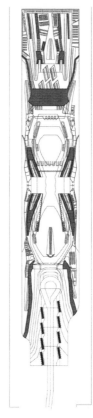
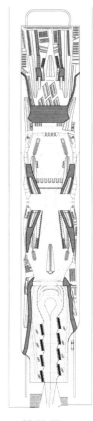

01.01.96   17.02.96   29.11.96   06.12.96   25.01.97   05.02.97

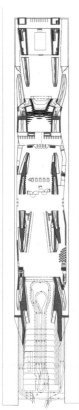

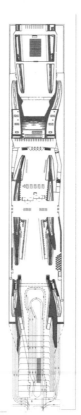
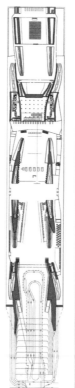
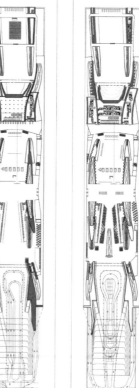
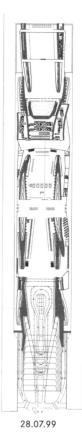

28.06.99   30.06.99   07.07.99   14.07.99   23.07.99   28.07.99

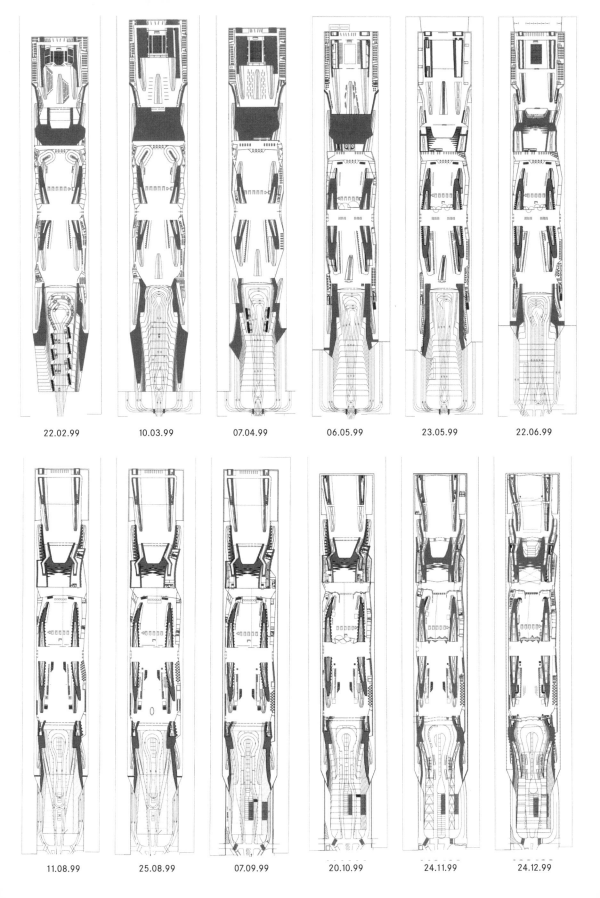

22.02.99   10.03.99   07.04.99   06.05.99   23.05.99   22.06.99

11.08.99   25.08.99   07.09.99   20.10.99   24.11.99   24.12.99

Structural girders   Roof folds

This is a very old model.
The geometry has changed since
then. Basically what we've done is
that the grid of the building
becomes constantly perpendicular
to the girders, so these folds
shift constantly, and the geometry
is no longer Cartesian.

An important research we have been involved in is to reduce the number of materials or details.
We have now 4 main details in the building – a steel detail, a wood detail, a glass detail, and a handrail detail – four basic systems which vary according to the changes in the geometry or functional requirements.

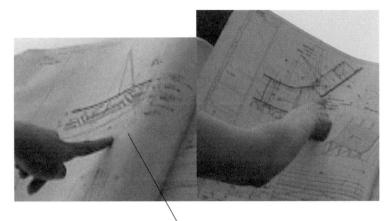

So the handrail detail at the edge is different to the one inside a ramp, or when it is collapsable to allow for the fingers to go on top of it.

The same with the wood
deck, in which the base
substructure is different
when it is outside and you
have to allow for drain, to
inside, where it is less deep
and has no insulation.

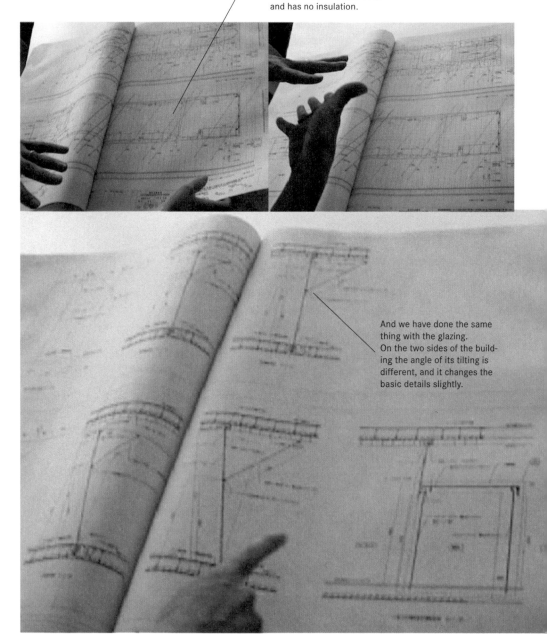

And we have done the same
thing with the glazing.
On the two sides of the building the angle of its tilting is
different, and it changes the
basic details slightly.

For example, we have different distances cantilevering at either edge (we must keep 3 meters for the cruise decks), and we have different programmes. In order to comply for all these requirements the tilt of the glass has to be different.

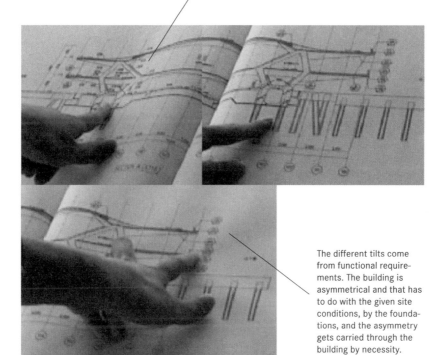

The different tilts come from functional requirements. The building is asymmetrical and that has to do with the given site conditions, by the foundations, and the asymmetry gets carried through the building by necessity.

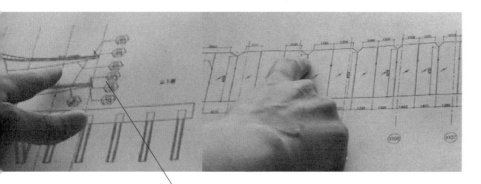

We used to have the folds of the structure come to the edge of the building. When the glass was cutting through the folds it would result in all these cuts, and that is obviously quite expensive.

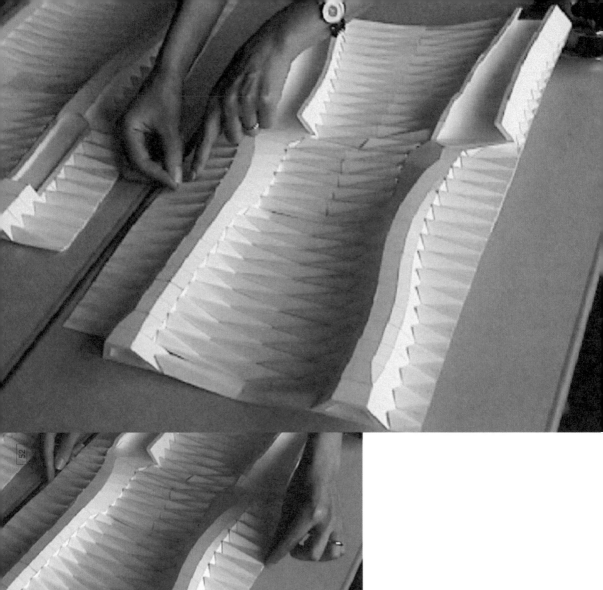

So what we've done is to stop the folds before, so that
when the glass meets the down surface of the roof it
meets a flat surface, thus avoiding all the cuts.
The edge is now obviously thicker to be cantilevered.
Then we also found out that structurally you could have
the folds throughout, but from a manufacturing point
of view any fold less than 3 meters long is impractical,
so they start disappearing now in some places.

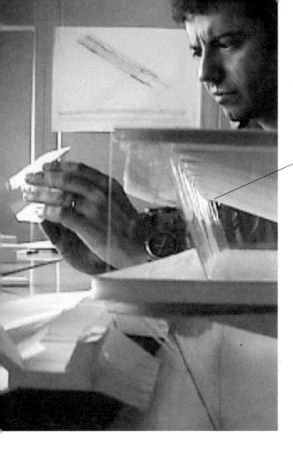

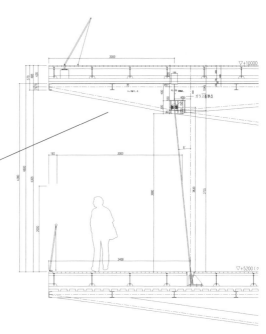

For the glazing structure we tested with rods, pipes, fins... all of these structures had to be modified to allow for this movement, for the different tilts, and it just became too heavy. The whole idea was to make this transparent, so we decided to go back to just glass, and see how much it can be tilted before you have to start adding structure.

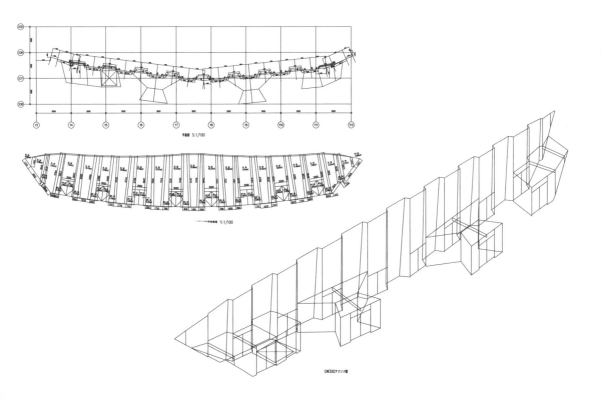

They are building the "mountains" now. The ground will stick out to raise the steel of the girders above the potential water level. Conceptually, we thought that rather than building a base for them...

...the foundations would stick out. The parking slab will be at the top of these beams, and that mesh that you see sticking out are one of these "mountain" shapes on top of which will sit the girders.

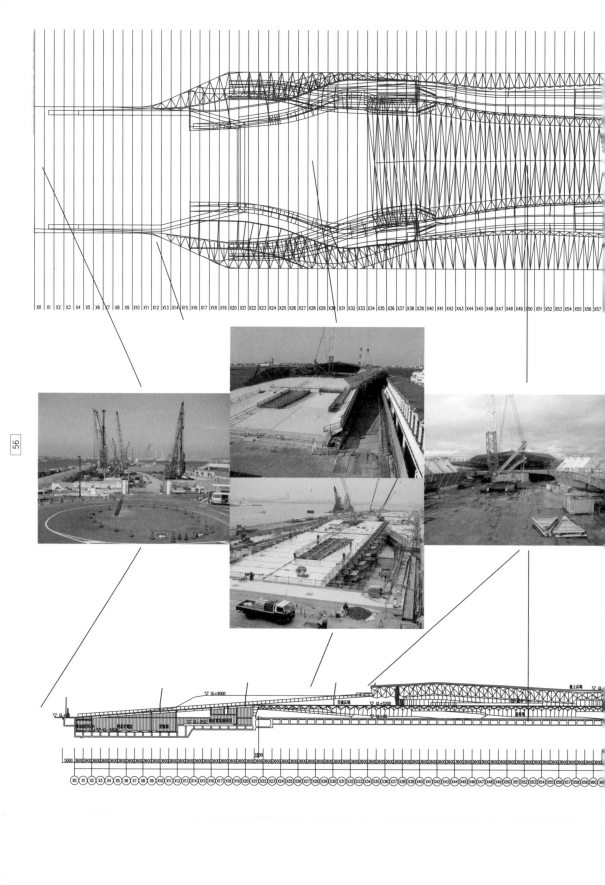

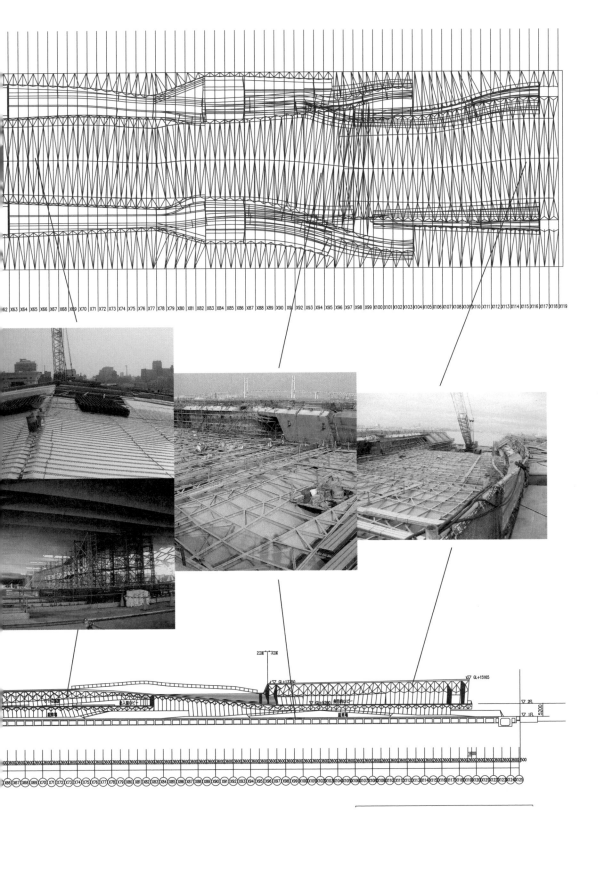

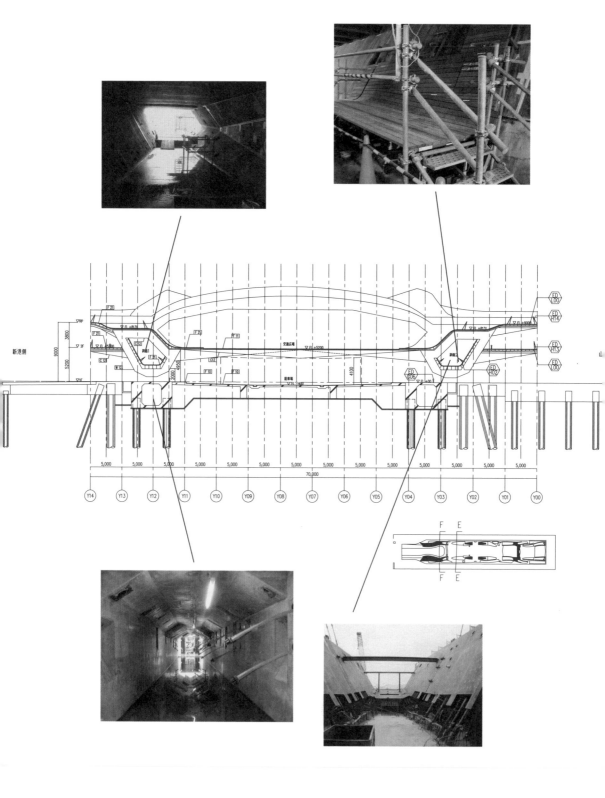

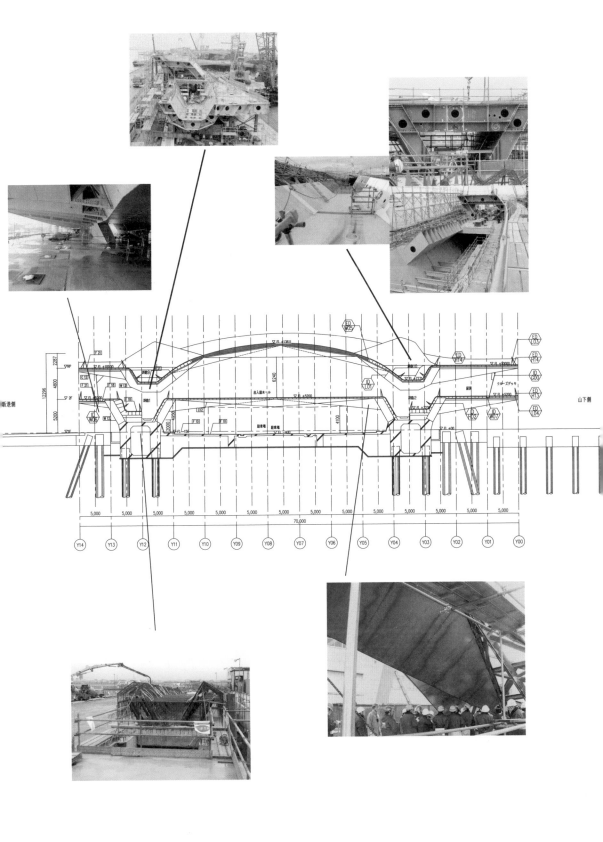

Connecting rods between
girders and ground

Within the girders, stiffeners are located appropriately to prevent buckling, but in the region for the supports where compressive forces are high, sections are also infilled with concrete to produce a hybrid structure.

Cross sections of girders

Stiffener connected to
concrete foundation

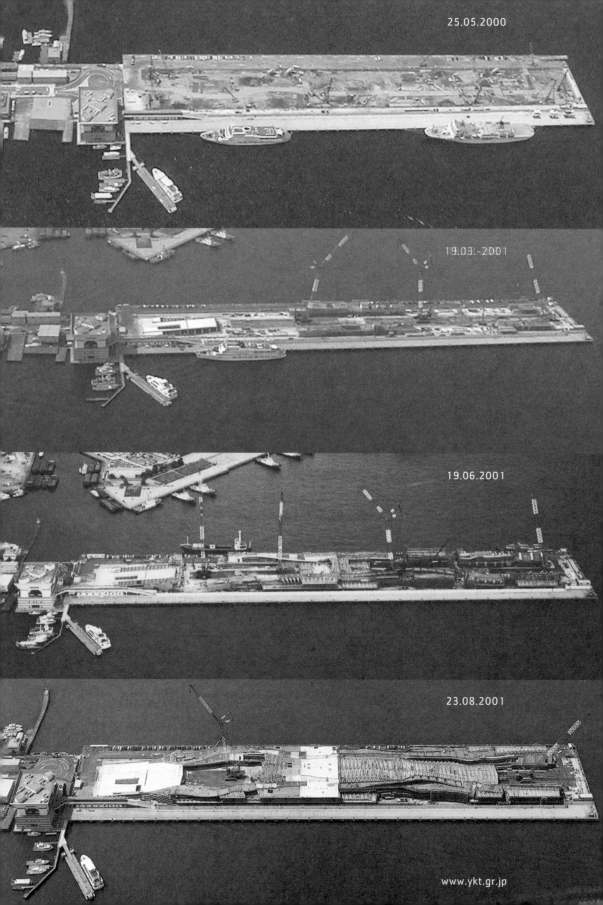

25.05.2000

19.03.-2001

19.06.2001

23.08.2001

www.ykt.gr.jp

To be continued...

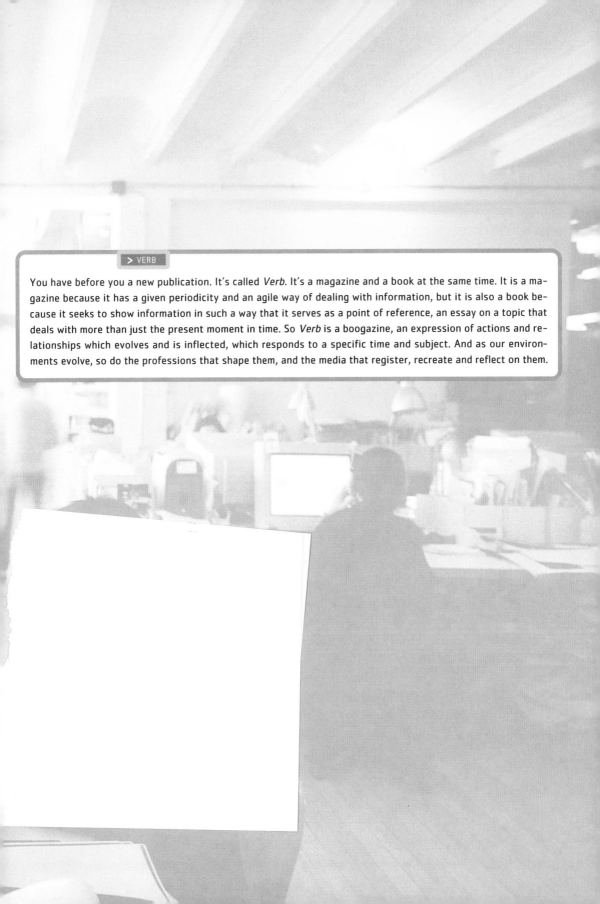

> VERB

You have before you a new publication. It's called *Verb*. It's a magazine and a book at the same time. It is a magazine because it has a given periodicity and an agile way of dealing with information, but it is also a book because it seeks to show information in such a way that it serves as a point of reference, an essay on a topic that deals with more than just the present moment in time. So *Verb* is a boogazine, an expression of actions and relationships which evolves and is inflected, which responds to a specific time and subject. And as our environments evolve, so do the professions that shape them, and the media that register, recreate and reflect on them.

DESIGN

WORK

USE

1

International Port Terminal, Yokohama
FOA, SDG
1994

10.1998

Yokohama Port Harbour Bureau
3.2002

86

Soundscape, Amersfoort.
Mossel, Vos, Witteman, Dean
10.1998

> VERB

We realize that publishing architectures is much more than displaying a recently finished product in which the architect is the unique author. To make architecture is a real undertaking — sometimes positive and sometimes frustrating for the architect — in which numerous authors participate and which is based on the processing of information before, during and after the materialization of the work.

92

Pavilion for
Expo Hannover 2000
b&k+
1999

+plattform@b&k+

102

Kölner Brett loft building
Cologne
b&k+
1997

1998

1999

116

Urban hybridization process.
Barakaldo
Nomad
10.1998

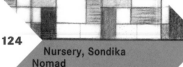

124

Nursery, Sondika
Nomad
1997

9.1997

7.1998

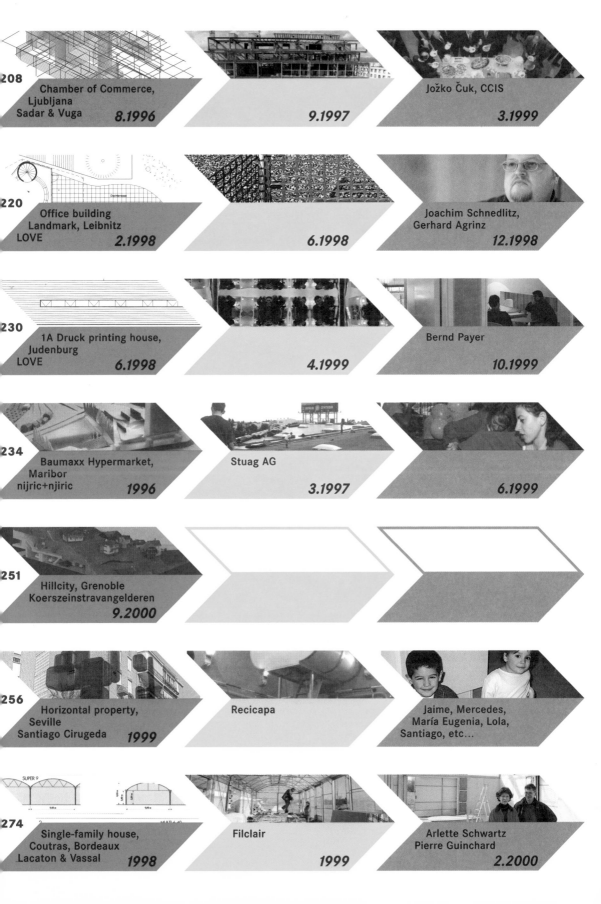

208 Chamber of Commerce, Ljubljana
Sadar & Vuga
8.1996

9.1997

Jožko Čuk, CCIS
3.1999

220 Office building
Landmark, Leibnitz
LOVE
2.1998

6.1998

Joachim Schnedlitz,
Gerhard Agrinz
12.1998

230 1A Druck printing house,
Judenburg
LOVE
6.1998

4.1999

Bernd Payer
10.1999

234 Baumaxx Hypermarket,
Maribor
nijric+njiric
1996

Stuag AG
3.1997

6.1999

251 Hillcity, Grenoble
Koerszeinstravangelderen
9.2000

256 Horizontal property,
Seville
Santiago Cirugeda
1999

Recicapa

Jaime, Mercedes,
María Eugenia, Lola,
Santiago, etc…

274 Single-family house,
Coutras, Bordeaux
Lacaton & Vassal
1998

Filclair
1999

Arlette Schwartz
Pierre Guinchard
2.2000

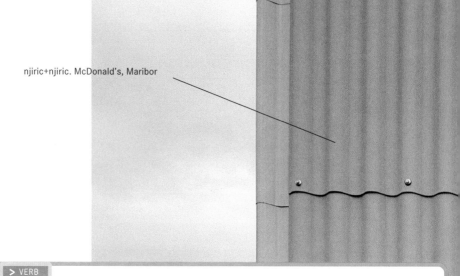

njiric+njiric. McDonald's, Maribor

> VERB

We work with increasingly interconnected computer networks, but how does this influence the content of professional practices? >>> We live in a time in which the processing of information is the basis of all material production. >>> Have only the tools changed? Or does content change too? >>> We are interested in seeing the influence this information processing has on the production of architectures. >>> We are trying to keep to the idea that the context of the information in which we work and live is open-ended, and independent of professions or of material practices. >>> Any data, any information can be useful to any practice. >>> Afterwards, it's the different producers — from architects to musicians, from scientists to publishers — who put this information into practice on their own area. >>> *Verb* is conceived as a means of communication between many actors, which tries to handle potential information in a fluid manner, one continually related to all other types of information about reality.

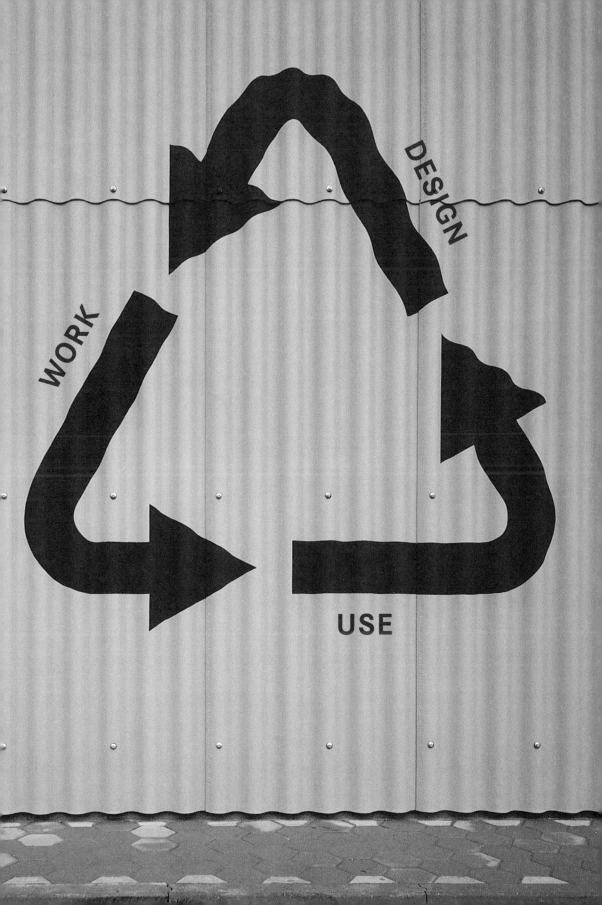

FOA, Yokohama `1`

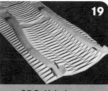

SDG, Yokohama `19`

TO THE LIMIT

Cirugeda, Seville
Horizontal property `261`

"Rollercoaster construc-
tion", Alejandro Zaera `13`

Conversation with
Farshid Moussavi `45`

Cirugeda, Seville
Inhabitable kit `259`

Lacaton & Vassal, Coutras
Glasshouse `274`

**UNDER
CONSTRUCTION**

LOVE, Leibnitz
Fast construction `222`

**PREFABRICATED
PRODUCTIONS**

njiric+njiric, Baumaxx
Ready-mades `244`

Sadar & Vuga,
Ljubljana `216`

LOVE, Judenburg
Faster construction `230`

Hillcity, Grenoble
Ordinary and banal `251`

njiric+njiric, Baumaxx
bricolage `248`

Sadar & Vuga,
Ljubljana `209`

LOVE brand `220`

MARKETING

njiric+njiric, Baumaxx
Hypermarket

Sadar & Vuga, Ljubljana
vernissage `219`

**FINISHED
WORK**

njiric+njiric, Baumaxx
Cake `234`

njiric+njiric, Baumaxx

For that reason, we present a bit of everything here:
Architects who attempt to translate parameters directly into buildable forms. Architects who, in not being able to build a project, redirect information about that project towards an experiment in interdisciplinary collaboration with artists, nuclear physicists or musicians. Architects who attempt to establish a kind of genome of an entire neighborhood, so as to later recombine that information in a different urban form. But not only are there experimental schemes. We feature those architects and others who build things too. Who seek in the technical market or in the dynamics of fashion and consumerism new ways of outlining a useful service as professionals. Or architects who work legally at the limit of what the norms permit. And also those who seek to develop a more direct, less underhand and less artistic relationship with the inhabitants of their architectures, basing themselves on the logics of *bricolage* and of "do-it-yourself". All this and much more, below...

266

Anton Markus Pasing
Science fiction

TV CULTURE

279

Lacaton & Vassal, Coutras
Client, inhabitant, author

USER

128

Nomad, Sondika
Learning

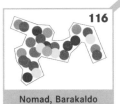

124

Nomad, Sondika
TV Advertising

DO IT YOURSELF

277

"36 models for a home",
Périphériques

MEDIA

126

Nomad, Sondika
"Al otro lado del espejo"

264

Verb to do

101

"in vitro landscape"
+plattform@b&k+

116

Nomad, Barakaldo
Urban hybridization

86

Mossel, Vos, Witteman,
Form follows Sound

102

b&k+, Cologne
Kölner Brett

92

b&k+, Hannover
Telematic landscape

DATA = FORM

89

Penelope Dean
Soundscape

COMPLEXITY AGAINST UNCERTAINTY

Jorge Wagensberg

A living individual is an object of this world that tends to conserve its own identity, independently from the fluctuations of the rest of the world (the environment). And the environment does indeed change. Adaptation is the ability to withstand the typical changes of the environment. Independence (or adaptability) is the ability to withstand new changes. Adaptation refers to the certainty of the environment, adaptability to its uncertainty. They are not the same thing. We could even say that more of the former means less of the latter.

The uncertainty of the world is its greatest certainty. So if there is one question worth asking, it is this: how can one stay alive in an uncertain environment? Perhaps the key to understanding biological evolution is not the concept of adaptation but that of independence. The idea is promising, because physics and mathematics, their laws and theorems, operate in terms not of adaptation but of independence. Let's give it a try.

There are three main families of alternatives, the first of which is passive independence. The simplest and most banal way of being independent is to isolate oneself. This is when the boundary is impermeable to any exchange of matter, energy or information. It is the worst way to be independent, because in this case the stern Second Law of Thermodynamics is irremediably applied and the system slips towards the only possible state, that of thermodynamic equilibrium, in other words, death. There are many ways of being alive, but only one of being dead. Nevertheless, life makes use of many good approximations to this alternative: latency, hibernation, resistant forms such as seeds, covering and simple growth (greater inertia)... The idea is to reduce activity or maintain simplicity, cross your fingers and wait for better times.

Jorge Wagensberg, PhD in Physics, is Director of the Science Museum of Barcelona

In active independence the individual opens itself out to the world in order to maintain a far-from-equilibrium steady state. The equations of the physics of open systems and mathematics of communication explain how this is done. If the uncertainty of the environment increases, independence from this state can be maintained either by increasing the system's capacity to anticipate (better perception, better knowledge...), or by increasing its ability to influence the immediate environment, i.e., through greater mobility (the ability to change environment) or more technology (the ability to change the environment), as in the case of nests and dens.

If active independence fails and the fluctuations of the environment are so wild that it is impossible to maintain a steady state, there still remains the possibility of new independence, that is, evolution. This is achieved through the combination of existing individuals. Well-proven strategies include reproduction (especially sexual, of course), symbiosis and other types of association. In this case, the equations are clear: an increase in the uncertainty of the environment requires an increase in the complexity of the system.

To progress in an environment is simply to gain independence from it. Progressive and regressive lines are not an example and a counterexample of the same contradictory event but two particular cases of a more general one. Regression occurs in conditions of hyperstability and progress occurs under the pressure of environmental uncertainty. We can breathe a sigh of relief and find reconciliation with the gut feeling that, after all, something happened between the appearance of the first prokaryotic bacterium and – shall we say – the birth of Shakespeare.

> VERB

This text is like a declaration of intentions. Wagensberg has a scientific background, but he is above all a communicator. He is one of those people who decode specialist information to make it intelligible to the rest of us. His contribution here is not science as such, but rather a reflection on scientific thought. He does not appear here for his in-depth knowledge in a specific field, but for his ability to create a connection between that knowledge and the knowledge of non-scientists. Just as he does, architects also decode. They are neither technicians nor scientists nor sociologists. They are translators. Translators of reality into constructible matter. And this is what we are interested in discussing here... how architects assimilate reality and translate it into constructible matter today.

Outskirts of Amersfoort

> VERB

Information is presented to us in the form of digits, parameters, statistics, data bases. Data processing and electronics form a kind of basic condition for any discipline. For example, the car itself is a hybrid of mechanics and electronics, and even of telematics. An ever more sophisticated mix of information processing and of matter. And architects — how can they translate that information into buildable matter? Can the acoustic or the telematic, or even the genetic, be turned into architecture, for instance?[1] What form can the relationships between matter and information take, right now?

Form follows sound. Tom Mossel, Casper Vos, Stefan Witteman

In the Netherlands, the demand for more space has increased considerably over the past ten years. Industry, infrastructures, agriculture and nature all claiming their share of the surface area. The Netherlands are threatened by overcrowding. It is therefore becoming necessary to build at higher densities. The landscape becomes highly monotonous: in the residential areas people only live, in the office spaces people only work and the agriculture and nature areas must be separated from each other and from the rest. A mixture of functions cannot exist because the rules in force (noise pollution, access to daylight, stench circles around farms), as well as municipal norms such as Development Plans, prevent them from doing so.

This separation of functions also makes it necessary to assign more space per function, as double use is not possible, and more and longer traffic movements must be made between the different functions, which leads to more infrastructure. To make density possible, functions must be able to mix. More constructed surface per hectare, more different functions per hectare.

Infrastructure occupies a lot of space. The legislation on noise pollution provides that a maximum decibel level must be assigned to a house or a permanent place of work. This means that no housing or high-rise functions may be accommodated within 1200 m of a motorway or railway. Because of the *ad hoc* nature of the development of these areas there is a lack of cohesion and people are faced with a low-quality result.

A possible solution that has been practised recently in many places in the Netherlands is to border a motorway or railway with anti-noise screens. However, this requires enormous investment in relation to the number of houses that benefit from them. It also impoverishes the landscape for the residents as well as for motorists and train passengers. The motorways and railways become a chain of anti-noise screens. How can we prevent the abstraction of the neighbourhood when towns and villages have to be recognised by their anti-noise screen? What are the implications of using the zones alongside the motorway or railway to obtain more density?

In the Netherlands these present a potential construction area of more or less 2640 km², about 6.4% of the total surface of the Netherlands. There is the possibility of creating a direct connection beside the motorway: living, work and recreation areas with a link to the motorway.

1 Experimental proposals by T. Mossel, C. Vos, S. Witteman, p. 86, b&k+, p. 92, nomad, p. 116

| 80 dB and less | 75 dB and less | 70 dB and less | 70-75 dB | 75 dB and more |

Noise scape. Penelope Dean

This is the data 'context' from which the proposal originates. A cubic vacuum is subjected to an 8-lane asphalt freeway of infinite length carrying a traffic intensity of 4000 vehicles per hour moving at 120 km/hr. The vehicles, comprising equal proportions (25% each) of light, medium and heavy vehicles and motorcycles, emit noise ranging from 80 dB to 68 dB within the cube. Maximum decibel to program parameters are independently assigned as organizational devices within the cube. The data limits housing to 65 dB, public space to 70 dB, retail and office space to 75 dB and parking as limitless. Figures are for outside noise conditions where program and related structures are compatible without restriction.

Percentages derived from a 'normal' city quantify public space at 40%, housing at 30%, office space at 15%, parking at 10% and retail space at 5%. This allocation is viewed as the optimum target for programmatic distribution within the cube.

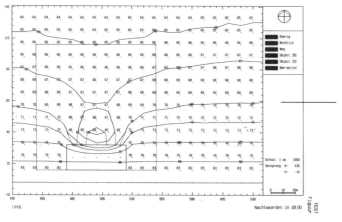

MVRDV: *FARMAX. Excursions on Density*, Winy Maas, Jacob van Rijs y Richard Koek (eds.), Rotterdam: 010 Publishers, 1998.

ACOUSTICAL RESEARCH: DGMR ARNHEM. This project is being developed at the Berlage Institute
NOISE SOURCE: 1. source: moving in unconfined locality – 0.75 m above ground; 2. freeway: 20 m wide – 8 lanes of two way traffic – symmetrical lane configuration – infinite length (calculations derived from 1000 m length); 3. traffic: speed of 120 km/hr – intensity of 4000 vehicles/hr (500 vehicles per lane per hour or one vehicle per lane per 7.2 seconds) – vehicles: 25% light, 25% medium, 25% heavy, 25% motorbikes; 4. road: asphalt; 5. ground: absorbent; 6. emission: as per Wegverkeerslawaai SRM 2 calculation program dgmr VL version 5.1/b.
DATA INTERPRETATION: Programmatic compatibility: 1. Decibel figures (dB) are for outside conditions where program and related structures are compatible without restriction i.e. insulation. – 2. The following maximum decibel/program compatibility figures are derived: housing 65 dB(A); public space 70 dB (A); retail space 75 dB(A); office space 75dB(A); parking without limit. – 3. Data operates as an organizational device for programs within the cube; Objective: Programmatic distribution – cube 100x100x100 m; 30 floors @ 3.3 m each; total floor area is 300 000 sqm.; Conclusion: 1. Excessive decibel levels vis-à-vis programmatic compatibility – 2. To program the cube, an obstacle needs to be introduced. Data design: 1. dimension 50 x 20 x100 m obstacle adjacent to freeway edge – 2. program: car park of 30 000 sqm – 3. effect: contours derived for 65 dB (A), 70 dB (A), 75 dB (A) 80 dB (A) at heights of +1.5 m, +25 m, +50 m, +75 m, +99.9 m.

Comfort zone. Tom Mossel, Casper Vos, Stefan Witteman

Applying the noise levels of the railway and motorway together with the need for access to daylight as structural principles, it is possible to determine the form of the comfort zone. The 65dB(A) noise level and the free daylight angle of 45° result in an urban sculpture, a hilly landscape within which it is possible to program without limits. This could be an advantage at a time when the borders between the different functions will be slowly disappearing. The urban layout can be fixed before the final program of the centre is determined.

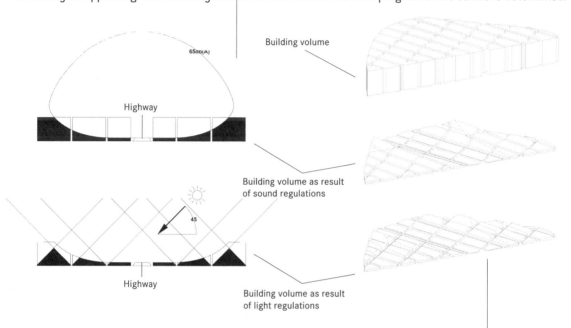

65dB(A)

Highway

Building volume

Building volume as result of sound regulations

45

Highway

Building volume as result of light regulations

The project proposes a transitional form between private gardens and areas of a collective nature. The traditional image of central parks and private houses with their own garden will have to be replaced by other forms of greenery such as vertical gardens, ivy-mantled houses, winter gardens and private backyards.

The structure of a private house should be interchangeable with that of an office. This subscribes to the development of offices with lower construction heights and the wish of dwellers to have higher ceilings. It makes it possible to combine domestic and professional functions (doctor's surgery-house, lounge-office, workshop-house, kindergarten, hotel-house, etc.).

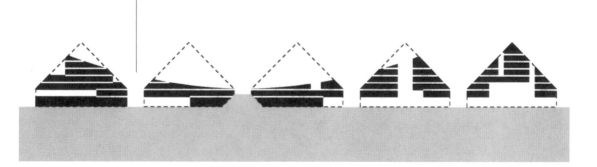

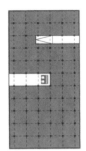

Level 0.
Shops/Supermarket

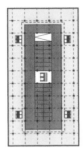

Level 1. Offices /
Parking

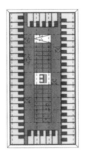

Level 2. Motel
Parking

Level 3-5. Housing

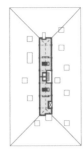

Level 6. Top flat

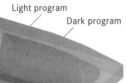

Light program

Dark program

The depth of the buildings
creates combinations of 'light'
and 'dark' programmes. Patios
and gardens bring daylight into
houses and offices.

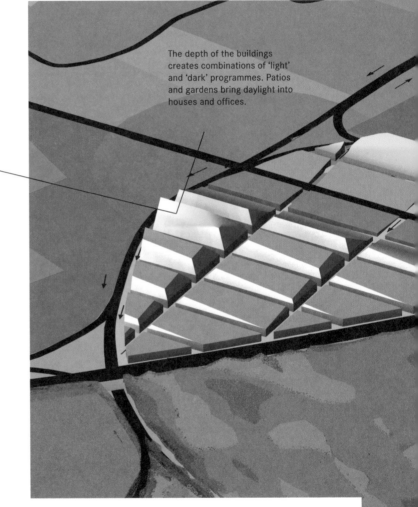

In this way, there will be less
traffic movement, a better
siting for companies, more
possibilities for public
transport, an improved mix
of functions.

Dodge   Library   McDonald's   SONY   School   IKEA

Housing   Housing   Housing   Park   Housing   Housing   Housing   Housing   Housing   Housing

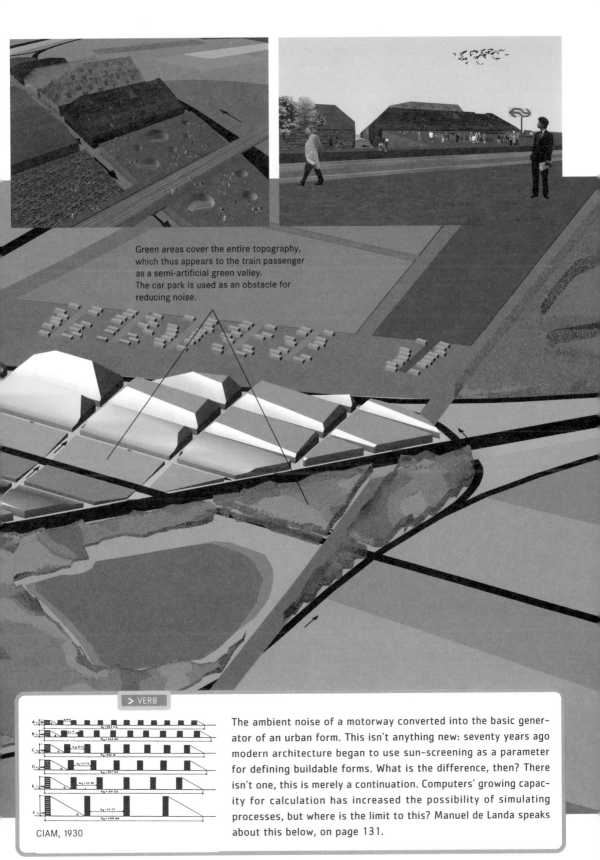

Green areas cover the entire topography,
which thus appears to the train passenger
as a semi-artificial green valley.
The car park is used as an obstacle for
reducing noise.

CIAM, 1930

The ambient noise of a motorway converted into the basic gener-
ator of an urban form. This isn't anything new: seventy years ago
modern architecture began to use sun-screening as a parameter
for defining buildable forms. What is the difference, then? There
isn't one, this is merely a continuation. Computers' growing capacity for calculation has increased the possibility of simulating
processes, but where is the limit to this? Manuel de Landa speaks
about this below, on page 131.

> VERB

Welcome to the world of the big company. How do you translate company information directly into an architectonic structure? This "telematic landscape" is an experiment. It attempts to find a way of constructing that information via a landscape midway between architecture and telematics. >>> In Summer 1998 the architects b&k+, the Global Human AG artists collective, and the designers of Casino Container began developing the idea of the "Telematic Landscape" as an open-ended interdisciplinary project. The origin of the project was a commission from an agency organizing events for a pavilion of a multinational company for the Hanover Expo that never got built.

telematischelandschaft.com

Bernd Kniess, b&k+ > We were interested in redefining the profile of a big multinational company without recourse to a specific representation of the product. We worked on various levels: firstly, its products. These extend from the high technology applied in satellites, via automobile electronics, to such common household appliances as drills and hairdryers. Secondly, the company system is paternalist and traditional, like a big family which trains its own employees at every level. Another important aspect is that it's a multinational that works in the shadow. Many of its products, above all in the automobile industry, are presented with the name of its clients. Lastly, we were to use the information as architectonic material. This meant imagining how we might build with information on different analogic, digital and media levels.

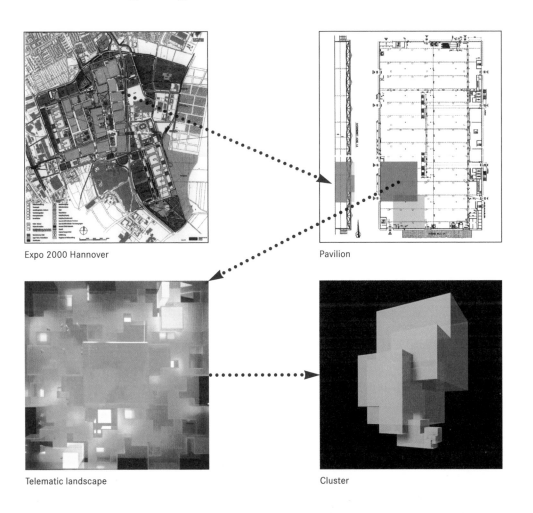

Expo 2000 Hannover

Pavilion

Telematic landscape

Cluster

b&k+ : Arno Brandlhuber, Bernd Kniess, Markus Emde, Ulli Wallner, Sven Bäucker, Meyer Voggenreiter (Casino Container), Rudi Frings (Global Human AG), Jochem Schneider

To perceive reality as a space-time continuum, extending from the miniscule to the vast, means creating a perception within a fractal form that exceeds the restrictions to our habitual perceptions of space. In opposition to an already unrealizable unitary vision, we must grasp that vision today is plural, diverse, fragmented and complex. This no longer involves moving in a purely mechanical sense, but in maintaining everything in an ongoing state of flux. The technological promise of telematics is based on sustaining, in every node, in every pixel, the quality of connection and of transmitted information. This is a qualitative leap from the mechanistic conception of the industrial era to the dynamic conception of networks, a system in which each pixel becomes intelligent. Each node is its own center. A content, a product is generated through this network. An architecture processor in real time, but without hierarchies. Via this processing of information and image, the apparatus becomes at once omnipresent and invisible. It vanishes: it's no longer a built object; it's become an "environment".

THE LANDSCAPE IS A FORM OF PERCEPTION

In defining our surroundings as a telematic landscape, we are referring to a type of landscape that generates itself instantaneously and continuously from the interconnection of natural and artificial forms, be these cultural, subjective or collective. The structure of such a landscape must be, therefore, indefinably self-referent and infinitely dimensional.

How is a virtual space generated, an enclave that isn't an enclave, seeing that it cannot be perceived within the Cartesian space of the industrial era, but in a different, computerized dimension in constant interaction with the viewer? On what models can such a construction be based?

www.telematischelandschaft.com

Bernd Kniess, b&k+ > We are seeking the way to fuse virtual and real space. The idea of projecting information on the walls of an interior-less "cave", in the form of a Moebius strip, is too unidirectional and impermeable to the action of the spectator. For this reason we are experimenting with other structures: amorphous space (generated from the macula of toroidal forms) and fractal space. The first has the same problems as the Moebius structure, so we're continuing experimenting with the fractal structure.

MOEBIUS
Where does the Moebius strip begin? With endless structures, the question immediately arises of where is the beginning and where the end.

CAVE
The physical construction itself of a virtual space plays a secondary role. It isn't the important thing. If we think of fictitious constructions like the holographic deck (holodeck) of the Enterprise, capable of generating an almost perfect artificial world from a totally anodine space, or in what might perhaps be the "purest" form of virtual space – the dream or the "trip"; frequently unrealizable without the aid of external agents – which goes way beyond, in its absolute structural freedom, any possible technology, we observe that we can't attempt to proceed from a physically stable, defined structure in order to create an artificial virtual world.

STRUCTURE 1: AMORPHOUS SPACE
A space generated from the macula of multiple tori results in an amorphous and undefined space in which the observer can only wander indefinitely without being able to fix his attention on a fixed point. A world without corners or edges, in which near and far dissolve into an almost absurd plane, at once flat and deep.

Mœbius strip

Klein Bottle

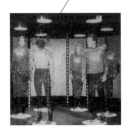

Holodeck

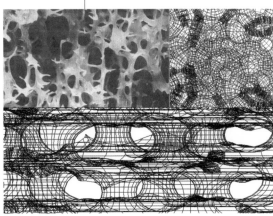

Telematic landscape I. Doughnuts

Telematic landscape II. Fractal

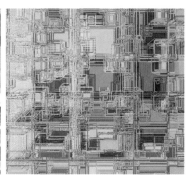

STRUCTURE 2: FRACTAL SPACE

If we look for the minimum unit, the basic building element of nature, we get fractals.

The telematic landscape must be self-generating.

For this reason, it is governed by a certain kind of information and a number of laws that cannot be understood, however, as a "command" in the strict sense of the word. Rather, this involves behavior patterns concerning the form, consistency and also the connectivity of the basic building cell, the fractal. The definitive form that arises from this process, if we can indeed speak of a final form, will be the telematic landscape itself.

A space structured this way doesn't seem to be a good support for the bits of information projected on it. In opposition to traditional projection, in which the observer's position has no great importance since it doesn't influence the action, in this fragmented fractal space it must be the observer himself who recomposes the images. For that reason, he must assume an active part in the flow of information.

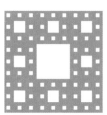

Telematic landscape II. Menger-Sierpinski

Telematic landscape III. Diagrams of spatial structure

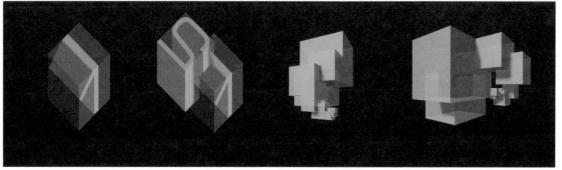

| Basic bicube | Combined bicube | Developed Cluster | Cluster, n-dimensional |

STRUCTURE 3: TELEMATICS

The word "telematics" has to do with simultaneous distance and proximity. If we eliminate distances we can project objects onto a single plane, independently of how far or near they are, they being only differentiable through their textures.

THE TELEMATIC LANDSCAPE

A different form of landscape is thereby created. Unknown, but also easily recognizable through our own experience. All we see, all we touch on, strikes us as strange and familiar at the same time. We must slightly modify our perception, but we accept that form, we go with it, we ourselves are our only reference, we define our own speed. In this moment the telematic landscape is our only ambient reality.

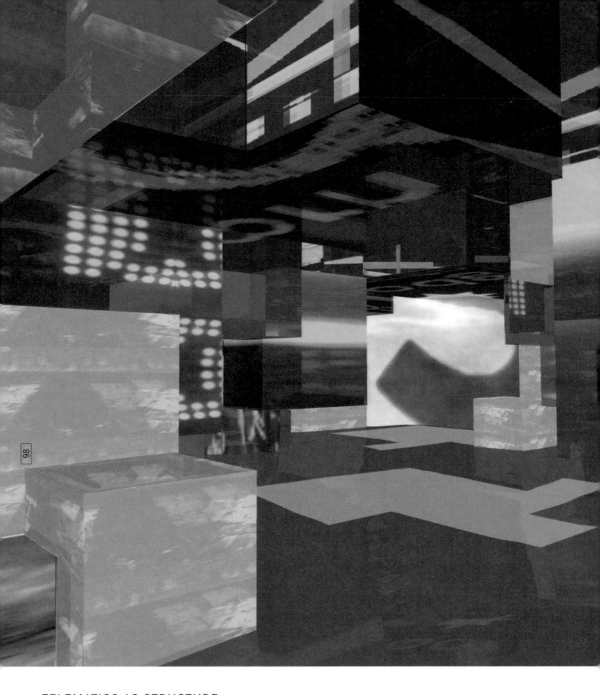

TELEMATICS AS STRUCTURE

The telematic landscape develops from one extremity to the other, from the unimaginably small to the infinitely large. It extends beyond the limits of what we can comprehend, but cannot really commence with 0 and end in the infinite, for all that. Where are its limits? We need a reference, a starting-point from which to understand where we are. We use that which, with complete safety, we can identify as a fundamental, integral part of the concept of "landscape", the tree.

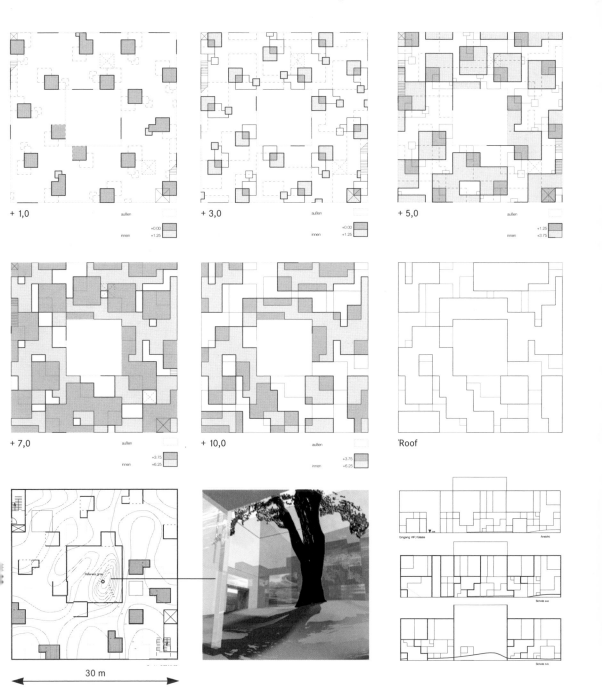

+ 1,0   außen

+0.00
innen   +1.25

+ 3,0   außen

+0.00
innen   +1.25

+ 5,0   außen

+1.25
innen   +3.75

+ 7,0   außen

+3.75
innen   +6.25

+ 10,0   außen

+3.75
innen   +6.25

'Roof

30 m

This was to have been the version set up, the telematische landschaft.com. But it never happened.
information that was gathered another project springs up, a non-constructional interdisciplinary
with different actors –physicists, choreographers, media theorists, artists, composers, gallery-own
ducers– which can be prolonged in time, the telematische landschaft.org.

telematischelandschaft.org

Actors > bittermann&duka, artist, Berlin; Jacopo Bonfadio di Gazano, scholar, Genoa; Andres Bossard, sound arc
Zurich; Casino Container, graphic designers, Cologne; Jean Chaize, choreographer, dancer, Berlin; Thomas Demand
Berlin; Christopher Dell, musician, Cologne; Vilém Flusser, philosopher, Paris; Global Human AG, artists, Cologne /
Meyer Voggenreiter, designer, Cologne Franz Müller, Boris Sieverts, artists, Cologne; N55, artists, Copenhague; O
artists, Berlin; Roxy Paine, artist, New York; Christiane Paul, media specialist, New York; Otto E. Rössler, nanophy
Tübingen; Uwe Schnatz, artist, Altmühltal; Jochem Schneider, theoretician, Stuttgart; Alice Stepanek, Steven Masli
Cologne/ Berlin; Mats Theselius, Daniel Hiorth, Andreas Roth, artists, Stockholm; Axel Wirths, media activist, Colo

One of the key ideas of the telematic work context is that material practices and professions are re-imbricated after centuries of separation. How do they work? How do architects get on with scientists, scientists with artists, artists with sociologists, sociologists with designers, designers with nuclear physicists, nuclear physicists with media people, media people with architects, etc?

telematischelandschaft.org is a prototype, auto-experimental initiative relating to the future conditions and practices of cultural producers. The concept of cultural producer is understood here in general terms, and reflects the change of the work world from a series of hierarchicized structures to others that are more liberalized and self-determining. The observer's status must also be clarified. The project's field of action and that of all the participants is, of course, the computer network. The structure of the work and the timing of the research project is organized by the "+plataform" and is structured in the following way:

¬ an interdisciplinary research group made up of approximately 15 professionals, among whom a post as observer is defined;
¬ a program of work and a data bank in Internet with which all members of the research group remain in contact, and which at a given moment also becomes known to the public, the idea being that the public take part in the process;
¬ regular workshops, which the different members organize in turn;
¬ after two years, a report about the research and an exhibition generated by the work program and using the data bank in Internet.

B&k+, in vitro landscape, Grundlagen zur Architekturgenetik [Bases for an Architectural Genetics], Book/catalogue of the exhibition in vitro landscape at the Weissenhof Architecture Gallery, Stuttgart, May-July 1999.

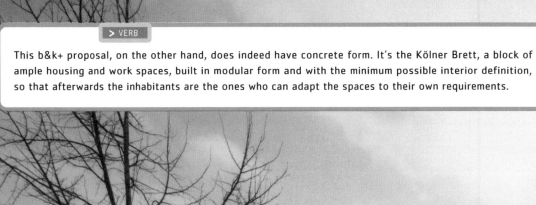

> VERB

This b&k+ proposal, on the other hand, does indeed have concrete form. It's the Kölner Brett, a block of ample housing and work spaces, built in modular form and with the minimum possible interior definition, so that afterwards the inhabitants are the ones who can adapt the spaces to their own requirements.

www.bk-plus.de

Am Kölner Brett

After producing this book, b&k+ have published another one on the "Politische Landschaft" workshop (www.political-landscape.org), which took place in Cologne in September 2000 in collaboration with Wuppertal University, the MAK (Museum für Angewandte Kunst in Cologne), the magazine *Arch+* and studio schoenerwissen. They have also published the CDs "Metazoon" by Christopher Dell and "Kölner Brett" by To Rococo Rot. They both have electronic music compositions – audio data – that relates to the architectural data from the following building in Kölner Brett.

Ehrenfeld neighborhood, Cologne

Helmholtzstrasse

The new global information technologies substantially change the bases of our closest surroundings, livable or otherwise.

Closeness and distance have lost their spatial dimension, a tendency that is also growing in family and couple relationships.

Social changes generate new forms of living and working.

The city calls for a greater quality of density.

The model based on fixed couple and family relationships, or on a stable job, is broken up into a series of temporally defined life situations.

The plot of land is found in an urban area undergoing reconversion. Despite their proximity to the center, the heterogeneous buildings and urban uses elicit a sensation of the periphery.

In such surroundings, a building operation is proposed which accommodates a new layout of uses that normally only arise in "loft" form in already-existing industrial or commercial buildings. The combined offer of habitable and working space within an ample, but also differentiated, space is mainly directed at creative people in the art and media fields.

The structure of the spaces develops in modular form. The building volume consists of twelve identical spatial modules that are placed one on top of the other by means of gyrations or mirror symmetries. The basic area of the module is one-third of double height (with optional deck), and two-thirds of single height in the others. In the lower part is the bathroom and kitchen zone.

Proceeding from the basic multi-use units, a high degree of floor-plan flexibility and spatial diversity is created via the core's possibilities for horizontal and vertical connection.

Set options are offered for later on-site personalization: three different bathroom units exist, in which the positioning of the fittings can be decided by the user. The verandas can be disposed according to pre-established support points, in accordance with the client's wishes. A detailed catalogue offers these possible individual options.

The interiors are subsequently turned into specialized areas by the use their inhabitants impress on them: a dental prosthetist has his laboratory, engineers their office, a photographer, an interior designer and a lawyer use them as apartments, and two couples try out, in three joint units, possible ways of living and working in common.

The entrances occur in the ground-floor rear facade, via the gallery that juts out independently of the building, and also directly from the driveway.

This gallery and exterior balcony offers a wide range of possibilities. Areas are created that appear like little gardens, with garden furniture and planted flowerpots. The tops of the trees create the illusion of a park, with the green roof, terraces and fences.

The construction of the block was implemented by means of self-bearing panels of site-poured concrete and prefabricated concrete panels. The jutting volume is a monolithic construction of reinforced concrete realized with high-resistance formwork.

In the main and rear facades, the combination of large sliding mechanisms and horizontal folding panes allow for opening and ventilating all the interiors in an individual and more than adequate way. The glazing is resolved by means of plate glass with solar protection. The tops of the deciduous trees to east and west offer additional shade in the summer months.

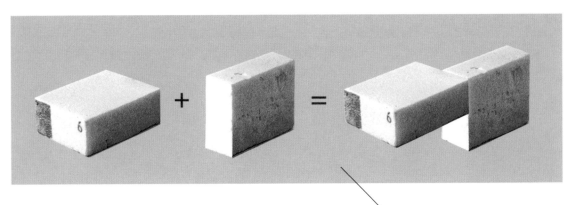

The building volume consists of twelve identical spatial modules that are placed one on top of the other by means of rotations or mirror symmetries.
The basic area of the module is one-third of double height (with optional deck), and two-thirds of single height in the others.

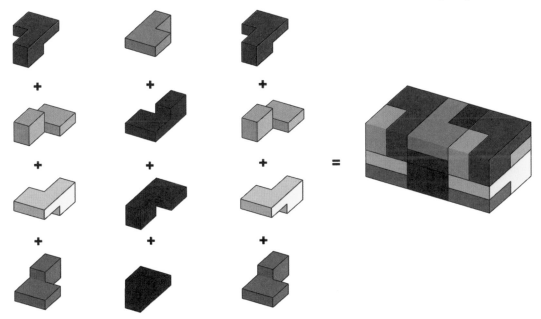

HOUSING-LOFT KÖLNER BRETT

Housing units: 12, partially on two levels. Usable surface area per unit: 140 m². Total floor area: 1,660 m². Usable space: 5,800 m³. Cost: € 1,687,263 (incl. VAT).
PROJECT, construction management: b&k+ Brandlhuber & Kniess + Partner, Cologne. Arno Brandlhuber, Bernd Kniess, Jörg Lammers, Lutz Löllmann, Ann Lüdecke, Bernard Schumann. Client: Ortner, Schultze, Mertens GbR. Structural engineering: Führer Kosch Stein, Aachen. Foundations: Jacbo, Weeze. Construction: Peters, Aachen. Facade: Peters, Aachen. Roofing: Peters, Aachen. Exterior installations: Peters, Aachen. Metal structure: Brendel, Cologne. Parquet: Thürnau, Bonn. Dry-assembly construction: Heller, Cologne. Tiling: Heller, Cologne. Electricity: Schiffer, Bergheim. Sanitary installations: Sühl, Cologne. Photographs: Michael Rasche, Lukas Roth and Stefan Schneider.

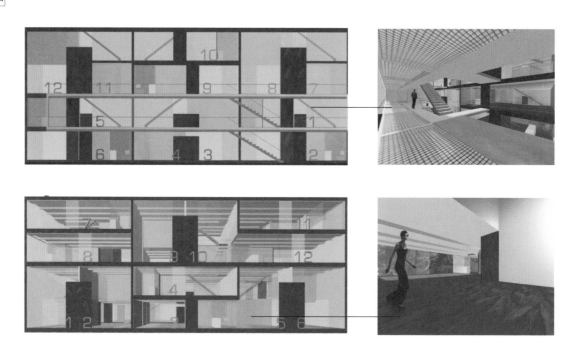

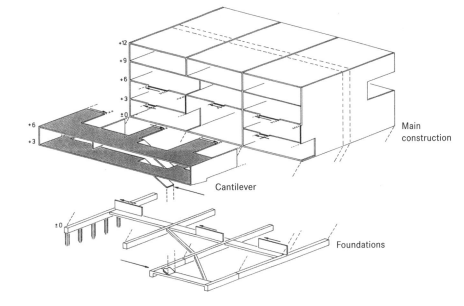

+12
+9
+6
+3
±0

+6
+3

Main
construction

Cantilever

±0

Foundations

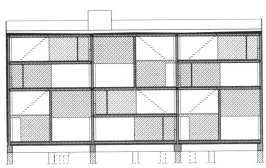

section 1

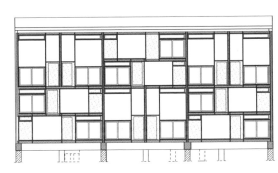

section 2

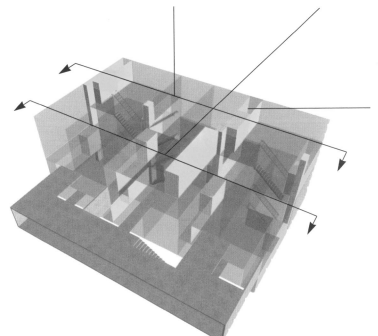

Sanitary modules:
3 variations
2 WC and washroom
WC, washroom and shower
WC, washroom and bath

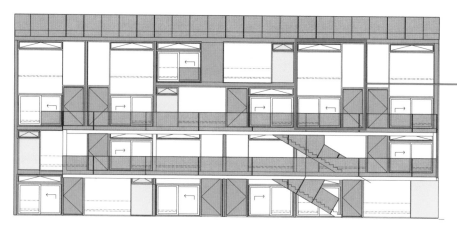

Gallery elevation (NE)

Interior view on pages 114-115

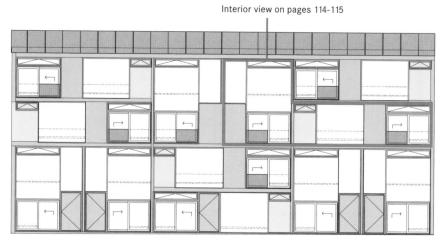

Helmholzstrasse elevation(SO)

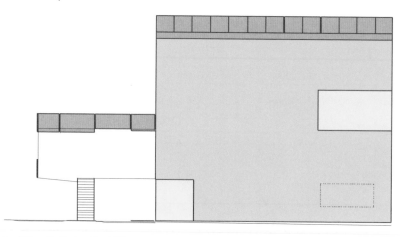

Am Kölner Brett elevation (NO)

4,70 m

0,60 m

3 m

5,70 m

3 m

2,10 m

"Alles, was Resopal ist".
Süddeutsche Zeitung,
21/12/2000

"b&k+'s juggling with the building turned out to be so
convincing that all the lofts have been sold long ago.
Meanwhile, each space has taken on a different aspect,
each interior amounting to a unique creation."

The main facades consist of sheets of insulating glass in gilded, anodized aluminum or galvanized steel frames, and slightly tinted sheets of translucent reinforced plastic

The exterior handrails are of reinforced plastic

29,50 m

26,10 m

110

The roof garden consists of 20 m² of lawn and concrete slabs

12,00

The side walls are sheets of glass and sheets of reinforced plastic with ventilation lower down

9,00

12 m

6,00

3,00

2,80 m

0,00

The decks are of site-poured concrete, with beams of pre-stressed concrete. The load-bearing walls are constructed of plain, natural gray, site-poured concrete with extensive smooth formwork.

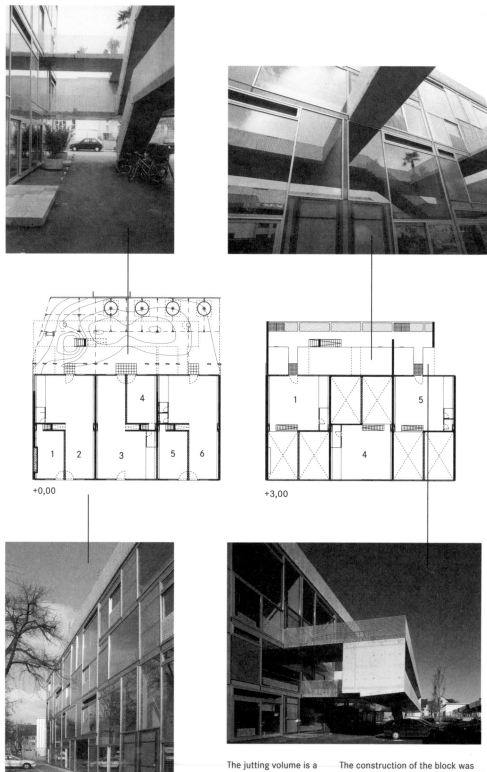

+0,00

+3,00

The jutting volume is a monolithic construction of reinforced concrete realized with high-resistance formwork.

The construction of the block was implemented by means of self-bearing panels of site-poured concrete and decks of prefabricated concrete paneling.

This gallery and exterior
balcony offers a wide range of
possibilities. Areas are created
that appear like little gardens,
with garden furniture and
planted flowerpots.

The tops of the trees
create the illusion of a
park, with the green roof,
terraces and hedges.

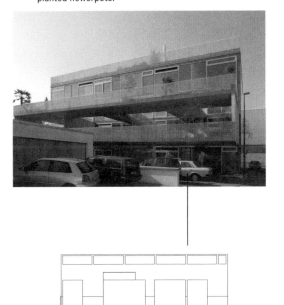

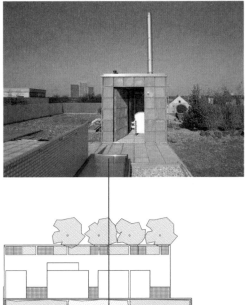

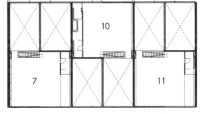

+9,00

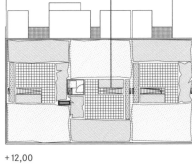

+12,00

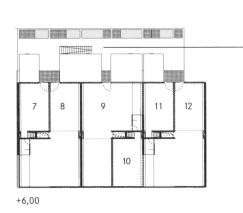

+6,00

Three-circuit electrical installation and exterior lighting, double plugs every 2.4 meters along the bare concrete walls

The heating consists of lacquered tube radiators with thermostat in different sizes and positions (on the facade at bench height), and the central boiler on the roof

In the main and rear facades, the combination of large sliding mechanisms and horizontal folding panes allow for opening and ventilating all the interiors in an individual and more than adequate way. The glazing is resolved by means of plate glass with solar protection. The tops of the deciduous trees to east and west offer additional shade in the summer months.

Each outer-wall unit consists of two 210 x 150-cm sliding doors and three case windows

2,70 m

The floors are of oak parquet

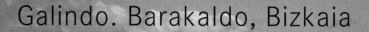

Galindo. Barakaldo, Bizkaia

Residential limit

Highway

Ring road

Water limit

Football stadium

Existing road

Railway lines

Green area

Visuals

Barakaldo connection

Existing buildings

Visual

Reality vectors

> VERB

How, and to what extent, can matter be broken down in computer terms? Can we work with urbanistic information in a way similar to genomatics in its computer handling of living matter?

This proposal is also experimental. It attempts to establish something akin to basic information about the matter of a new neighborhood. A series of theoretical parameters are negotiated using data drawn from reality. Archives thus emerge that are like chains of molecules of buildable and non-buildable matter.

A landscape is generated in this way, too. And in order to generate an informational-constructional landscape it's necessary to make a profound study of matter's innermost secrets.

Program   Proposed usage program

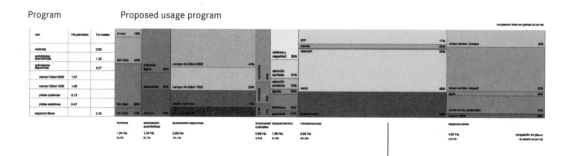

This is a process of landscape occupation that provides a release from compositive burdens from the outset.
REPLICATION: The first step of the process is to create an objective percentile distribution of the usage program to be inserted into the territory. These uses lead to individual grids that distribute each function uniformly, defining different densities of usage, from the percentile information about the total area of their point of application.
MUTATION: The second analysis determines the pre-existing factors and future actions considered to be unchangeable. The interaction between these reality vectors and the previous distributions of each function is used to produce a tabulation of attraction and repulsion between the latter. As a direct consequence of this two-way tug, there is an individualized shift and hence a mutation of densities until they reach equilibrium, relocated in their final points of installation in the landscape.

Interaction with reality vectors

	Housing	Economic activities / Sport activities	Cultural activities	Community facilities	Infraestructures	Leisure area

Further reading Ian L. McHarg: *Design with Nature*. John Wiley & Sons Inc., 1992.

u+wc 00.66%	2d+2wc 01.86%	3d+2wc 03.10%	4d+3wc 00.58%	industria ligera 03.35%	almacenes 01.34%	oficinas 02.01%	pistas cubiertas 03.74%	pistas exteriores 02.16%
comercios 02.04%	cafeterias 00.85%	cines 00.51%	equipamientos 05.50%	aparcamientos 08.85%	zonas verdes: bosque 04.84%	zonas verdes: césped 11.80%	agua 01.18%	zonas duras peatonales 04.84%

Percentage of densities

↓

Mutation of densities

COHESION: Once the balance of mutations is reached, the construction uses and open spaces are defined and grouped, leading to the configuration of the constructed hybrids.

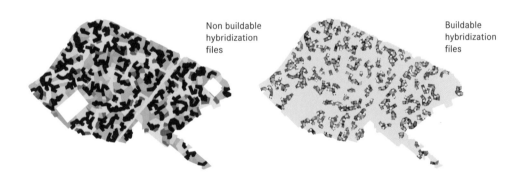

Non buildable hybridization files

Buildable hybridization files

TRANSCRIPTION: One result of this accumulation and identification of elements, superimposed in different ways, is a variable hybridization density of the territory, installed with the appearance of a statistical landscape of possibilities.

The recreation of this occupancy system in time takes pre-existing factors and their chronological duration into consideration, thus extending the hybridization process to ten years, beginning with the resolution of the built-up boundaries of Barakaldo and spreading to the railway lines and the Galindo River in a homogeneous colonization of the site.

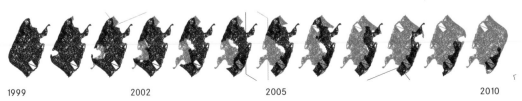

1999   2002   2005   2010

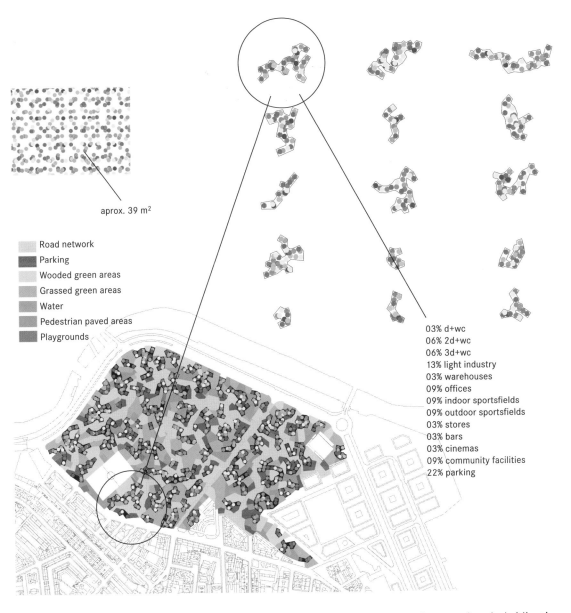

aprox. 39 m²

Road network
Parking
Wooded green areas
Grassed green areas
Water
Pedestrian paved areas
Playgrounds

03% d+wc
06% 2d+wc
06% 3d+wc
13% light industry
03% warehouses
09% offices
09% indoor sportsfields
09% outdoor sportsfields
03% stores
03% bars
03% cinemas
09% community facilities
22% parking

HYBRIDIZATION: By this means we reach the first result of the process: the complete hybridization of the landscape, an organization that takes into account all pre-existing elements with no formal planning goal, and which contains all the information required to create an anti-segregationist morphology of the city.

Once the territory is hybridized by the multiplicity of programmatic functions, it proceeds to read the constructive accumulations to create an archive of hybridization in which the percentages of participation on each function in the composition of the built unit can be read.

The primigenial volume arises from a simple calculation of areas, potential constructions and the superimposition of uses on the plan. This virtual volume is transformed by the environmental conditions that are fed in as values of installing this construction in the real built-up landscape. These conditions

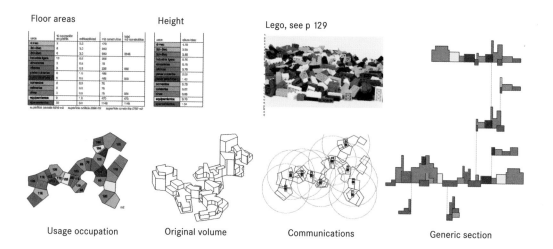

Floor areas Height Lego, see p 129

Usage occupation   Original volume   Communications   Generic section

are: accessibility of uses from the public level, heights of each use or placement of minimum communications cores to meet fire regulations.

The generic section of the building appears during this transformation, which is typified using the information on functions, relationships between them and their built volumes.

This functional hybrid is configured with green zones, dwellings, light industry, civic infrastructure, etc. The choice is a city in which uses are not segregated and distances are minimized physically and not technologically. This intermingling with the landscape extends the public land either partially across the constructed roofs or as a penetration of the constructions for vehicles or pedestrians, producing interactions with the surroundings. We thus characterize both the plan-level organizations arising from the symbiosis of the interior and the environment, as well as the voids and filters in the facade which respond in different ways to each differentiated use of the open space. In this idea of a pleasant, transitable city with little spatial privatization, the urban hybrids describe their functions

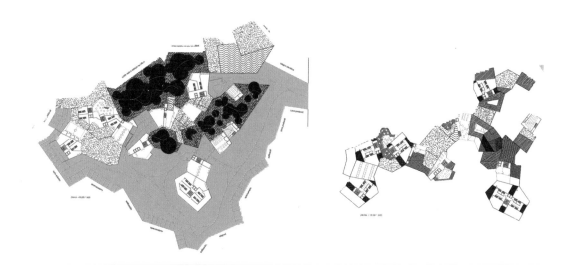

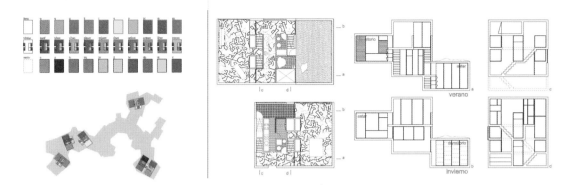

to the exterior by means of keys and codes of differentiated materials and colors aimed at enhanced identification and comprehension.

The environmental conditions, as with the definition of the urban hybrids, play a decisive role in the development of the dwelling and its means of relating to the exterior. The voids are the direct translation of a functional code of external uses found outside each facade (green areas or itineraries), giving them a greater or lesser degree of privacy.

The multiplicity of personalities and the hedonism of modern individuals, their habits and their increasingly atypical mobility and communication patterns make their dwellings extremely variable and heterogeneous places. From this point of view, we propose units that release architecture from its predominantly organizational function, moving instead to the level of support for the representation of potential lifestyles.

> VERB

Everything is related. Matter is not so inert as it seems, and ultimately the design of constructible matter can depend, to a great extent, on a more in-depth processing of the information. Scratching deeper into the reality of things. A little deeper. Genetics, nanotechnology, artificial intelligence. We are discovering that the matter of which we are made can be decoded and processed. And then we are involving hitherto inert matter in encoding and learning processes that give it life. So where's the limit? Where are we heading?

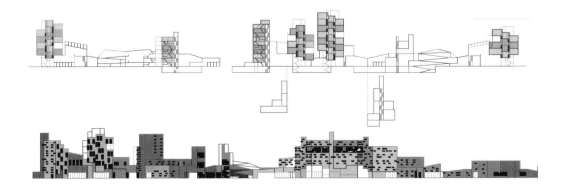

Thoughts on Architecture during Television Commercials

Anton Markus Pasing

TECHNOLOGY

Nobody can deny that technology is a good thing. How we use it is another matter. Everybody talks of cyberspace and virtual reality, internet and rendering, but there are remarkable aspects which are rarely attended to in architecture. Take for instance the possibility of supporting personal likes or dislikes through technology. Why don't we start with something that we can all do, like lying. Lying helps us through life, more or less. Any medium will do. One thing we can do is to let our answerphone tell callers that we are out, while we are at home, secretly. Or we can feed those calling with other false information. That's brilliant, but it by no means exhausts the technological potential for all manners of illusions and dishonesties. We need programs (let's call them Jokers) that talk to unwanted persons on the phone, calming them so that they, in the end, put down the receiver quite satisfied. This would require rhetorically trained programs that were also fed with the most important data of the phone extension owner.

Things will become really interesting with videophones. For these we need a perfectly animated 3-D-picture that will add to the caller's satisfaction and be able to generate a poker face as required. This means that we create a kind of avatar for ourselves, a highly specialized one. Translated into architecture it will then be possible to build up the dishonesties we have so far carefully cultivated to an utterly fictitious existence. Both Disneyland and, to some extent, Robert Venturi will assist us in this as the great models they are. We will build a 'decorated shed' (pages 230, 246) for ourselves, this time with all the latest technical gadgets and not as honest, not by a long shot. I'm not thinking of Las Vegas' Sunset Strip, no that would be much too true, but rather of Disneyland. I'm thinking of the perfect illusion, both subtle and credible. In a preliminary phase we could, for example, replace windows and conservatories by monitor screens. These new windows will help us to present a sane world or a sound family life to the outside, while inside we can rant and rage and do immoral things. In order to make the family perfect we then need a holographic system that projects happy and well-fed children playing in the garden, when we don't have any children, or perhaps we do, but they're unhappy. And maybe we don't even have a real garden.

It is also possible to replace entire façades by flat screens so that, seen from outside, our house seems to comply with building regulations while in the interior we can do whatever we want. Or else we use the screens as a kind of magic cap to become invisible. That is the negation of presence. The rejection of building mass. Absolute privacy by way of a perfect lie. Finally, we can now build where we're not really allowed to build. Anarchy? Truth? Or only the logical development of ongoing trends? Nothing changes except the electricity bill. Welcome home!

ARCHITECTURE

What exactly does architecture consist of? Is there something like the prime matter, or essence of architecture? Can a house have a soul? What exactly makes a house a home? Is it the objects it contains, the people who live in it, its stones or secrets – or just our childhood memories? Architecture certainly is all that is stable, gives space, keeps the weather and the poachers out – but is that all? Is there anything else beside the building materials, whatever they may be? If there is, will we be capable of recognizing it? What are the things we remember about a city we have visited? The blue sky, the nice or else unfriendly people we met, the city's architecture – or just the shop window displays? But let's return to the protoplasm of architecture and assume that apart from the building blocks of stone, steel, glass and timber there are other, immaterial building blocks. What would these consist of? Supposing we built a parallel world by computer and 'played God', i.e. made everything new?: Thoughts are building stones.

Let us begin. Of course, we need residents. These could be humans, animals, but also androids, robot babies, mutants, clones, parasites or God-knows-what. Here we go! Roofs, we need roofs – and spaces. But how do we go about it? Let's imagine a house consists of a balance of forces, so forces need counterforces. Stairs are good examples for this. A stairway or path can only be experienced by means of muscles producing body movement. So I simply design counter-muscles. These need floorspace. In order to define this area as a three-dimensional space so that we can experience it in walking through it in time, I need a time-space. I need to picture how my organism wishes this space or room to be. Of course it has to have the potential for change, because we, too, change all the time. I must have a holodeck [page 95]. If I have one space, I can have all space. What exactly does the holodeck run on? I know it just at this moment, just for myself, of course, and only for a few seconds. Never mind, perhaps already tomorrow seconds will turn into days. If everything can change, then one has to reckon with the laws of physics changing, too. This means there is not just one least common multiple in the holodeck, but there are many.

Some of these least common multiples are stories, personal fates and fortunes consisting of hate, cynicism, dreams, dissatisfaction, disappointment, power, hope, fun, desire, love and death, imaginings, toys and many a skeleton in the cupboard. But that is nothing to build on, to build with – one might think. What else do we have? Stones, steel, timber, plastic and glass are stupid. They don't know where they fit and belong, they are dead matter – or are they? Does architecture really only mean ideas? Can thinking be replaced by building? Building through thinking.

Who influences whom, and by which means? Is there a free play of forces? Demurely learning from our television culture we zap through pictures of foreign worlds, thereby making foreign pictures our own or using foreign images to create new ones instead of digesting our own experience. Discovering means inventing. We drift along and are the remote-control and the television actors all in one. Everybody influences everybody else. The only important thing is to feel that it is we who control the perfect meta-instrument, i.e. the remote control. Less important is the fact that we have long since ceased to be the ones who choose the channels we watch. We dance from one channel to the next as in a great ballet of different worlds and create our own choreography of the Now. From these mechanisms we also create the architecture which we designers promote since we participate in the culture of building.

To what extent are everyday culture and architecture coherent? Where will the people live who today dance to Techno, Ambient, Jazz, Drum and Bass? A huge effort must be necessary to make these people feel at home in a newly built German housing development. Or will they just turn up the music, buy designer clothes, shut their eyes and dream of fantasy worlds or clear spaces?

Never mind, let's leave it at that. The film will continue in a minute. Everybody will get what they deserve. Stories are projects, with words, people and their lives as the real building blocks. We are all building the city, consciously or unconsciously. What happens though, if the drive from a higher to a lower energy level, common in physical nature, also applies to thought? Money and greed. CAD instead of IQ. Every effort in vain. Stupidity carries the day, does it? Perhaps it does. The play instinct is all part of it. Trial and error. That's o.k. It can't turn out much worse. So there, let's experiment, and laugh from time to time. There are more important things than architecture!

...the commercials are over. The film goes on.

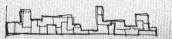

From Barakaldo...

→

to Sondika.

Sondika

Images from the ad "Frisbee", made by the production company Tesauro for Retevision

"We had to find locations for a television commercial. In Vitoria we stumbled across an exhibition on the latest architecture prizes in the Basque Country. With the addition of the odd attrezzo element, the nursery became the house we were looking for."

Tesauro, television production company

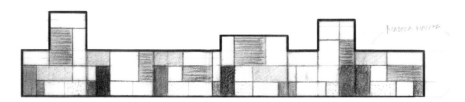

KINDERGARTEN COLEGIO VIZCAYA. Carretera Sto. Domingo-Derio km 6. Sondika, Bizkaia.
<u>Total floor area:</u> 427 m². <u>Total built area:</u> 395.34 m². <u>Budget:</u> € 259.000 VAT incl. <u>Design:</u> NOMAD arquitectura,
Eduardo Arroyo. <u>Supervision:</u> Eduardo Arroyo, Pedro Paz (surveyor). <u>Structural engineering:</u> Joaquín Antuña, Ignacio Avila (architects).
<u>Contractors:</u> Lomsa, Pablo Jiménez (surveyor). <u>Electricity:</u> Skorpio, Patxi Hernando (Product engineer)

Eduardo Arroyo. *Al otro lado del espejo*

The east-facing picture window takes advantage of the gentle morning sunshine and relates the interior to the playground

6 m

Vizcaya school

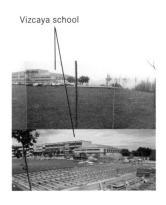

French school

Hall	10,42
WC teachers	7,0
Kitchen	8,33
Teachers area	34,86
Multiple area	85,55
Corridor	36,66
Classroom A	40,24
Classroom B	41
Classroom C	41,25
Classroom D	29,17
Classroom E	29,30
Bathroom	8,76
WC A	4,5
WC B	9,24
WC C	9,24
Total built area	395,34 m²

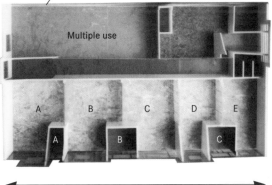

Multiple use

15,50 m

27,50 m

Epure-type inwardly folding
windows by Technal

Climalit-Plus double window (exterior:
6 mm Planilux + 8 mm dehydrated air
space + interior: 6 mm low-emission
Planitherm with perimetral double seal)

PG-type doors by Technal with 30-cm
lower blind baseboard, doors and
windows received on iron pre-frame

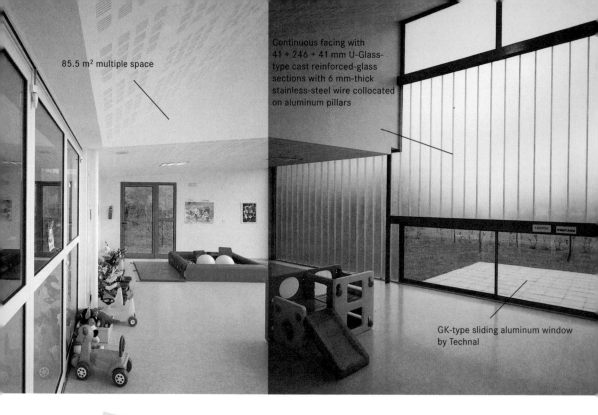

85.5 m² multiple space

Continuous facing with
41 + 246 + 41 mm U-Glass-
type cast reinforced-glass
sections with 6 mm-thick
stainless-steel wire collocated
on aluminum pillars

GK-type sliding aluminum window
by Technal

The nursery's promotional catalogue

Classroom D: 29,17 m²

The west-facing translucent wall allows the late-afternoon light to be glimpsed and creates an increased feeling of protection

The floors are of natural linoleum

LEGO DECALOG: 1. Unlimited possibilities of play; 2. For boys and girls; 3. Exciting at all ages; 4. Playable year-round; 5. A stimulating and absorbing game; 6. Endless hours of play; 7. Imagination, creativity, development; 8. Each new product multiplies its value; 9. Always up-to-date; 10. At the highest levels of safety and quality. Published in *Domus 819*

Washroom: 9.24 m²

Verb > The more experimental schemes seem to confirm that with computer processing the idea of authorship in architecture not only doesn't disappear, but becomes more widespread. Architects still design and decide, but in another way. Modernism is raised to the power of ten… It's as if we were moving architectural design towards information about clients, needs, building standards, energy flows, construction materials and techniques and so on; all that data that was more or less invisible until just a few years ago. But what does it all mean?

Manuel de Landa > In Deleuze there is a distinction between two ways of producing forms, in nature or in society: one imposes a previously existing form on a material that is regarded as inert (the hylomorphic schema[1] in his terms), while in the other, forms are given to an active material, without imposing it. This issue, which in a way indicates two types of authorship, matches perfectly with that of self-organization, bottom-up development, etc. But it can also be linked to computer design. In my work, using the programs Wavefront and Maya, I have come to realize that this difference in paradigms for the genesis (or authorship) of form is reflected in different types of software (specifically, solid modelling vs. particle dynamics software). These examples could serve me to bring together a more general essay on the relationship between information and authorship.

Verb > Do you think we'll reach the point of autonomous information processing, such as a software package that designs and builds without the need for an "act of authorship"? Or is it rather that authorship now has a lot more information to act on, to design with, and that this transforms the idea of design and authorship into something different, something that can no longer be defined in the same way as it was up to now?

Manuel de Landa > My point of view in the essay would be that authorship has always had several differentiated forms, because there is a non-human as well as a human agent in the production of form. Nevertheless, certain forms of software (such as genetic algorithms that make it possible to "breed" beings) do actually change the type of agency or authorship. Do you think we'll reach the point of autonomous information processing, such as a software package that designs and builds without the need for an "act of authorship"? Or is it rather that authorship now has a lot more information to act on, to design with, and that this transforms the idea of design and authorship into something different, something that can no longer be defined in the same way as it was up to now?

---

1 *Hylomorphism* (from *hyle*, matter and *morphé*, form) is an Aristotelian term, according to which natural objects are irreducible components.

PHILOSOPHIES OF DESIGN

THE CASE OF MODELING SOFTWARE

MANUEL DE LANDA

Manuel de Landa has lived in Manhattan since 1975, although he was born in Mexico City. He began as an independent filmmaker, but he's mainly known for his books and essays about non-linear dynamics, theories of organization, intelligence and artificial life. He's the author of `War in the Age of Intelligent Machines´ and `One Thousand Years of Nonlinear History´. Although he doesn't write about design, he works, paradoxically, as a designer doing 3D modeling by computer.

Further reading, see Manuel de Landa, "Deleuze and the Open-ended Becoming of the World"
www.diss.sense.uni-konstanz.de/virtualitaet/delanda.htm,
www.brown.edu/Departments/Watson_Institute/programs/gs/VirtualY2K/delanda.html

The widespread use of steel for so many purposes in the modern world is only partly due to techni- cal causes. Steel, especially mild steel, might euphemistically be described as a material that facil- itates the dilution of skills... Manufacturing processes can be broken down into many separate stages, each requiring a minimum of skill or intelligence... At a higher mental level, the design process becomes a good deal easier and more foolproof by the use of a ductile, isotropic, and practically uniform material with which there is already a great deal of accumulated experience. The *design* of many components, such as gear wheels, *can be reduced to a routine* that can be looked up in hand- books. One consequence has been that managers and accountants, rather than engineers, have become the dominant personalities in large organizations. Creative thinking is directed into rather narrow channels. Steel is, archetypically, the material of big business —of large factories, railroads and so on. James E. Gordon [1]

In this essay I would like to contrast two different philosophies of design, or what amounts to the same thing, two different theories of the *genesis of form*. In one philosophy one thinks of form or design as primarily conceptual or cerebral, something to be generated as a pure thought in isolation from the messy world of matter and energy. Once conceived, a design can be given physical form by simply imposing it on a material substratum, which is taken to be *homogenous*, obedient and recep- tive to the wishes of the designer. Steel, as the opening quote of this essay claims, is one such docile material, with predictable qualities and standard behavior. Although such a philosophy may seem nat- ural to some designers, there is the danger that utilizing materials with routine behavior may end up affecting the design process itself, reducing it, at least in part, to yet another routine. The opposite stance would be represented by a philosophy of design in which materials are not inert receptacles for a cerebral form imposed from the outside, but active participants in the genesis of form. This implies the existence of *heterogeneous* materials, with variable properties and idiosyncrasies which the designer must respect and make an integral part of a design process which, it follows, cannot be

1 James Edward Gordon. *The Science of Structures and Materials*. (Scientific American Library, 1988). Page 135. (My Italics).

routinized. I will illustrate these two opposite attitudes towards matter and form with examples from real materials first, and then move on to examples from virtual materials, that is, the "matter" inside computer simulations which is the basis of Computer Assisted Design (CAD).

The author of our opening quote, James Gordon, was one of the pioneers of the science of materials, a new field of science born in the 1950's from the conjunction of many separate areas: metallurgy, polymer science, glass and ceramics engineering, solid state physics and other minor fields. Thus, Materials Science and Engineering, as the field has come to be called, was from its inception *inherently interdisciplinary*. Gordon argues that, despite the importance in this century of new materials for economic and military purposes, none of those fields ever enjoyed a great deal of prestige, certainly nothing like the prestige attached to relativity or quantum physics. The reason for this humble status is directly related to the two philosophies of design I will be discussing. Real material behavior is complex, demanding an interdisciplinary approach, but science traditionally has looked down on such collaborative efforts. Hence, the complex behavior of materials has been typically neglected and reduced to simple, routine properties. The physics developed by Newton stripped materials of all their complexity and reduced them to "mass", while the chemistry which developed a century and a half later, dealt only with the simplest chemical properties and interactions.

On the other hand, craftsmen (blacksmiths, glassmakers, shipbuilders) always had to take the complexity of matter into account because before the advent of homogenized materials like steel, the materials available were always heterogeneous. A blacksmith, for example, would get his iron from one mine one week, from another distant one the following week, from a meteorite later on, each time dealing with different impurities and mixtures that demanded creativity and did not allow the process of creation of new forms to be reduced to routine. But precisely because the knowledge of complex material behavior was in the hands of craftsmen (and later on, of architects and engineers) there was a general disregard for it. Western societies, all the way back to their ancient Greek origins, have traditionally despised manual knowledge. Blacksmiths in Greece, for instance, were typically slaves or ex-slaves, and were regarded with suspicion by Greek citizens (even those who enjoyed metallic designs for ornament or weaponry) for spending their days surrounded by fire and dealing with metals, and more importantly, for not coming to the Agora to talk and discuss issues of citizenship and other high-minded subjects.[2]

The blacksmith had plenty of knowledge, but it was *linguistically unarticulated knowledge*, know-how embodied in his hands, not the kind of knowledge that can be easily verbalized and made into con-

2 Melvin Kranzberg and Cyril Stanley Smith. "Materials in History and Society." In Tom Forester editor. *The Materials Revolution*. (MIT Press, 1988). Page 93.

versation or put into books. Know-how, as opposed to linguistic or mathematical knowledge, has never enjoyed any prestige and has been largely ignored by philosophers as a worthy subject of study. Today, thanks to Artificial Intelligence, this situation may change: we know now that getting machines to learn verbal knowledge (or any kind of formal knowledge such as that involved in playing chess) is a great deal easier than creating a mechanical hand that can design and create metallic objects. In other words, the type of knowledge that we always thought was the most characteristic of human rationality, and hence, what made us different from animals and machines is, in fact, the easier to mechanize. And the minor, less prestigious skills which we have always neglected to study, are the hardest to transmit to a machine, hence, the least mechanical.

Yet, Artificial Intelligence is rather new and has hardly begun to alter a contemptuous attitude towards manual skill and complex materiality which is rather ancient. Moreover, this attitude has been formalized and embodied in specific philosophies such as *creationism*. God, the architect of the world, creates form by first thinking about it and then imposing it on matter as a command: let there be light, let there be form. Form is thought to be primarily *conceptual*, an idea in the divine designer's mind, and the process to embody this mental design is seen as similar to giving orders in the military, that is, a process which assumes instant obedience. One does not, of course, have to believe in creationism to subscribe to this philosophy. *Platonic essences* (eternal ideal forms inhabiting some other world) perform the same function as God's thoughts. In both cases, the origin of form is *transcendental* with matter deprived of any active agency and reduced to a willing receptacle.

Yet, as Gilles Deleuze has shown, not every Western philosopher has adopted that attitude. In philosophers like Spinoza, Deleuze discovers another possibility: that the resources involved in the genesis of form are *immanent* to matter itself, not transcendental. Materials have an inherent capacity for the generation of form, an inherent ability to self-organize in certain conditions. The simplest case of this capacity is illustrated by the phenomena of *phase transitions*. This is the scientific term to refer to the spontaneous changes which occur in the structure of materials at certain critical points of intensity, such as the condensation of steam into liquid droplets, or the crystallization of water into ice, at critical points of temperature. During these phase transitions, matter spontaneously changes architecture, from the gaseous structure of steam to the very different spatial organization of a liquid, to the more rigid architecture of a crystal lattice. Metallurgists in the past knew about these phase transitions in metals and knew that *how one crosses the critical point matters*. For instance, once one melts the metal it matters how fast one allows it to solidify, whether one lets it air-cool slowly or whether one accelerates the solidification by quenching it, submerging it suddenly into cold water. In one case one ends up with a more perfectly crystalline material (air-cooling allows the molecules to take their time finding their right place in the crystal lattice) and in the other case with a more amorphous, glass-like material (quenching does not allow the molecules to organize into regular arrays). For at least a thousand years before philosophers like Aristotle began their speculations, most of the knowledge about metallic phase transitions, and about the mixture of different metals (such as copper and tin) to get novel properties (in alloys such as bronze) was developed on a purely empirical basis, through a direct interaction with the complex behavior of materials. Indeed, the early Greek philosophies of matter may have been derived from observation and conversation with those "whose eyes had seen and whose fingers had felt the intricacies of the behavior of materials during thermal processing or as they were shaped by chipping, cutting or plastic deformation."[3] For instance, Aristotle's famous four elements – fire, earth, water and air – may reflect his awareness (through his interactions with craftsmen) of what today we know as the three main states of aggregation of matter – the solid, liquid and gas states – plus the state with least structure, the plasma state represented by an open flame. Yet, despite their debt to those who worked with their hands, philosophers have tended to neglect craftsmen's own design philosophy and reduce it to essentialism or creationism. One reason for this neglect may be that the philosophy of design of metallurgists and other craftsmen was implicit (not verbally articulated). It nevertheless was a real alternative to both essentialism and creationism. Instead of imposing a cerebral form on an inert matter, materials *were allowed to have their say* in the final form produced. Craftsmen did not impose a shape but rather teased out a form from the material, acting more as triggers for spontaneous behavior and as facilitators of spontaneous processes than as commanders imposing their desires from above. In all this, there was a respect for matter's own form-generating capabilities and an ability to deal with heterogeneity. But is this other philosophy a thing of the past? Are we being romantically nostalgic about a golden age of non-routinized design procedures that are today inevitably lost? Or, on the contrary, is the era of steel (and other homogenized materials) only a passing phase which is about to be left behind by a renaissance of novel and more complexly behaved materials? James Gordon seems to think the latter alternative is more likely. The idea that a single, universal material is good for all different kinds of structure, some of which may be supporting loads in compression, some in tension, is what seems to be wrong. As in the case of biological materials like bone, new designs may involve structures with properties that are in continuous variation, with some portions of the structure better able to deal with compression while

3 Cyril Stanley Smith. "Matter Versus Materials: A Historical View." In *A Search for Structure*. (MIT Press, 1992). Page 115.

others deal with tension. *Intrinsically heterogeneous* materials, such as fiberglass and the newer hi-tech composites, afford designers this possibility. As Gordon says, "it is scarcely practicable to tabulate elaborate sets of 'typical mechanical properties' for the new composites. In theory, the whole point of such materials is that, unlike metals, they do not have 'typical properties', because the material is designed to suit not only each individual structure, but each place in that structure."[4]

The problem is that, despite the availability of new materials with complex behavior, our design skills may now lag behind. Many centuries of thinking about the genesis of form as occurring mostly in the brain without interaction with matter have deprived us of these skills. Or more exactly, since it is not just a question of an ideology shaping our minds, several historical processes have conspired to impose the wrong philosophy of design. For example, the nineteenth century process of routinizing labor, of transferring skills from the human worker to the machine (the process which came to be known as Taylorism) and the task of homogenizing metallic behavior went hand in hand. As Cyril Stanley Smith remarks "The craftsman can compensate for differences in the qualities of his material, for he can adjust the precise strength and pattern of application of his tools to the material's local vagaries. Conversely, the constant motion of a machine requires constant materials."[5] Given that much of the knowledge about the non-constant behavior of materials was developed outside science by empirically oriented individuals, the deskilling of craftsmen that accompanied mechanization involved a loss of that know-how. And since that loss was directly related to the needs of command and control, we have here an example not only of a philosophy of design but of a *politics of design*.

Gilles Deleuze has attempted to change the dominant philosophy of design, or more generally, the dominant philosophy of the genesis of form, by recovering some of the experience of the old metallurgists and developing it in a more abstract way. He uses the term "machinic phylum" to refer to the world of matter and energy when it is conceived without an architect God (or any other transcendental source of form, such as essences). By the term "machinic" he means simply "the articulation of heterogeneities as such", that is, the creation of form with materials that have not been made obedient by homogenization.[6] The term "phylum" he takes from biology where it means the category just below "kingdom". We as vertebrates, for example, belong to the phylum "chordata". But beyond being the name for a category, phylum means a particular body-plan, an *abstract architecture* from which we can obtain, via different embryological processes, a large variety of concrete architectures: if we fold and stretch a fertilized egg following a certain sequence we get a giraffe; follow another sequence, we get an elephant; yet other sequences yield all the different architectural structures of the other vertebrates.

4 James Edward Gordon. *op. cit.* Page 200.
5 Cyril Stanley Smith. *op. cit.* Page 313.
6 Gilles Deleuze and Felix Guattari. *A Thousand Plateaus.* (University of Minnesota Press, 1980) Page 329.

When the two words are put together, "machinic phylum" means that there is just one body-plan not only for animals, but also for plants, clouds, winds, mountains etc. All these different structures would, if Deleuze is right, stem from one and the same abstract architecture. One universal phylum would be divided into many more specific phyla, including the different lineages that make our technologies. Each phyla would be characterized by their phase transitions (which Deleuze calls "singularities") and by the properties which materials acquire as they cross those critical points (properties which he calls "traits of expression"). To quote him in full:

"Let us return to the example of the saber, or rather of crucible steel. It implies the actualization of a first singularity, namely the melting of the iron at high temperature; then a second singularity, the successive decarbonations; corresponding to these singularities are traits of expression –not only the hardness, sharpness and finish, but also the undulations or designs traced by the crystallization and resulting from the internal structure of the cast of steel. The iron sword is associated with entirely different singularities because it is forged and not cast or molded, quenched and not air cooled, produced by the piece and not in number; its traits of expression are necessarily different because it pierces rather than hews, attacks from the front rather than from the side...We may speak of a machinic phylum, or technological lineage, wherever we find a constellation of singularities, prolongable by certain operations, which converge, and make the operations converge, upon one or several assignable traits of expression. If the singularities or operations diverge, we must distinguish two different phyla: that is precisely the case for the iron sword, descended from the dagger, and the steel saber, descended from the knife... But it is always possible to situate the analysis on the level of singularities that are prolongable from one phylum to another, and to tie the two phyla together. At the limit, there is a single phylogenetic lineage, a single machinic phylum, ideally continuous: the flow of matter-movement, the flow of matter in continuous variation, conveying singularities and traits of expression."[7]

The design philosophy which a theory of the machinic phylum implies goes directly against the idea of form coming from the outside to shape an inert material, and implies a certain respect for the inherent shape-generating capabilities of matter. Speaking of the relation of carpenters to wood as an active material, he says "it is a question of surrendering to the wood, then following where it leads by connecting operations to a materiality [such as the variable undulations and torsions of the fibers guiding the operation of splitting wood] instead of imposing a form upon a matter."[8] Later on he adds that the machinic phylum can only be followed, not commanded into obedience. "Doubtless, the operation that consists in following can be carried out in one place: an artisan who planes follows the wood, the

7 Gilles Deleuze and Felix Guattari. *A Thousand Plateaus.* op. cit. Page 406.
8 Ibid. Page 408.

fibers of the wood, without changing location... [But] artisans are obliged to follow in another way as well... to go find the wood where it lies, and to find the wood with the right kind of fibers".[9]

The know-how and sensual knowledge characteristic of craftsmen then, needs to be placed in the context of a world where matter and energy (the overall machinic phylum) are full of capabilities to differentiate into a multiplicity of phyla (some geological, some biological. some technological) and where creative tinkering and trial and error can indeed track the lines of development inherent in the machinic phylum, test what happens when a material crosses a singularity or discover when a mixture leads to novel properties. As I said above, the availability of new materials which are inherently heterogeneous, such as fiber-glass and other composites, may allow designers to break with the old design philosophy and to "track the machinic phylum", in order to create structures with more complex behavior. But there are other recent technological developments, such as the availability of *virtual materials* within computers, which also demand this other attitude towards design. While the oldest forms of Computer Assisted Design (CAD) software conformed to the old paradigm, with each new innovation in CAD new virtual materials have been introduced which do not lend themselves so easily to a mere imposition of a cerebral design, and demand a certain interaction between designer and material. I would like to discuss here several of these innovations, including the use of flexible surfaces (Bezier or Nurbs surfaces), the use of flows of pixels endowed with a certain virtual physics (Particle Dynamics) and the use of biological evolutionary strategies to, in effect, *breed new designs* like one would breed a race horse (Genetic Algorithms).

The simplest form of CAD is called "solid modeling" software and involves a simulation of the simplest state of matter, the crystal. Liquid behavior is much harder to simulate, and gases and plasmas, despite their statistical simplicity, are also difficult, because they involve the deployment of thousands of small particles. Most early forms of solid modeling involved a simple "material", rigid polygons, and allowed only a few operations for the creation of basic shapes, such as taking a line representing the profile of a simple, symmetric shape (a wine glass or a bottle) and spinning it around to generate a three dimensional form. These are "surfaces of revolution", so called because they are generated by spinning or revolving a line. Another simple operation, called "extrusion", begins with a surface or a cross-section and generates a three-dimensional shape by displacing it or scaling it, while at the same time providing new side surfaces to complete the solid form. In both cases only a very small repertoire of shapes may be created. This reduced variety may be increased somewhat by including "Boolean operations", which allow the designer to combine several forms generated by revolution or extrusion.

9 Ibid. Page 409.

For example, one may carve out a round hole into a solid shape by using a cylinder and the Boolean operation of subtraction, which removes material from the solid shape in the form of another solid shape. All these primitive operations are standard in most CAD packages. They implicitly embody one of the two design philosophies I mentioned before: one basically imposes a form on a virtual material, rigid polygons, which is completely inert.

The first departure from the world of obedient rigid polygons was represented by special flexible curves called "splines". These curves already contain a kind of singular behavior. In this case, of course, a "singularity" does not refer to critical points defining a phase transition, but to the special points that define a curve, such as the inflection points at which a curved line changes direction. When curves are defined by their singular points (inflection, maxima and minima points) they become a little more "alive", a little more plastic, since one curve can be continuously deformed into another and will count as the same curve as long as it contains the same singularities. (We can think of these curves as deformable French curves.) When the same idea is applied to surfaces, the virtual patches inherit the flexibility of the curves and the designer must begin to respect some of the inherent behavior of these surfaces (called Bezier patches or in most advanced software, Nurbs, Non-Uniform-Rational-Bezier-Surfaces).

The basic idea behind a spline is that the designer does not specify every single point of the curve, but only a few key weights which deform the curve in certain ways. The software then displays the simplest curve, the one with the most streamlined shape, which matches those weights. One can, of course, add so many weights that in effect one is defining the curve at every point, but then one loses the streamlined form. In other words, the designer may impose his or her will at every point, defining the form in minute detail, but then the inherent tendencies of the spline to "seek" the most efficient curve are lost. And a similar point applies to surfaces: to take advantage of their intrinsic capacity to bend in the most streamlined way designers need to refrain from imposing too many constraints on them, else they might as well go back to the rigid, polygonal surfaces of the earliest CAD packages.

A more extreme departure from the old paradigm is embodied in more recent software, such as Particle Dynamics. The original purpose of this software was to generate forms which are not solid, such as fire, wind, snow, rain or any other mobile pattern which involves a large population of constantly changing small particles. Here one begins not with an obedient piece of clay which may be molded in any way one wishes, but with a flow of pixels which, in order to be shaped, must be caught in one of several available fields: a gravitational field, a vortex field, a turbulent field and so on. The pixels (or smallest picture elements) can be given a history specifying what happens to their properties (color, transparency) as they flow. For example, to create fire one begins with a pixel flow in which the color is specified to begin stark white (at the hottest point of the fire) and change slowly to yellow, orange and red. The transparency is also specified to begin fully opaque and end fully transparent, so that particles disappear as they get further away from the source. Finally, one traps this flow into a turbulence field and manipulates some knobs which specify certain properties (such frequency or amplitude) which determine how tame or wild the resulting flames will be. In this process, the designer is not imposing a predefined form but attempting to tease out or elicit the emergence of a changing form from a flow which has its own intrinsic behavior. Here the challenge for designers is to invent novel uses for this software, that is, uses which do not involve the simulation of fire or rain, but that go beyond these original applications.

But perhaps the greatest challenge to designers will be when Genetic Algorithms become a standard part of CAD programs. Unlike the two design tools I just described, this software was created not to aid designers but biologists in understanding the dynamics of evolutionary processes. Basically, the software allows the definition of a virtual form by a set of instructions, and the transformation of those instructions into the genes or DNA of the form. Then, the software allows those virtual forms to sexually mate with one another, recombining their instructions as they give rise to varied offspring. The Genetic Algorithm keeps track of what virtual form mated with what other form and which new combinations of genes are being produced with each generation, including random mutations in the instructions. When used as a design tool (as it has been done by artists such as William Latham[10]) the designer's role is to decide, at each generation, which forms will survive and which will die, or in other words, the artist's role is to *guide the evolution* of these forms. In performing this guiding task the designer becomes a kind of animal breeder: a dog or horse breeder can hardly impose a predefined form on his animals and at best plays the role of aesthetic (or functional) judge. In other words, the breeder selects which dogs or horses will get to mate with each other, crossing small dogs with small dogs, for instance, if the aim is to end up with a Chihuahua, or fast horses with fast horses, if the aim is to end up with a race horse.

But there is an important difference between CAD designers and breeders. Unlike someone manipulating evolution in the realm of biology, where one starts from the beginning with a fantastically productive phylum or body-plan (the body-plan of the vertebrates, for instance), in the virtual realm one does not have an abstract architecture full of potential, but *must create one*. The Genetic Algorithm,

10 Stephen Todd and William Latham. *Evolutionary Art and Computers.* (Academic Press, 1992).

in a way, does the easy part, to keep track of the recombinatory logistics of a large population of virtual forms. But if one does not start with a combinatorially rich body-plan (such as that of our own phylum or that of the phylum to which insects belong) the evolutionary process does not yield surprising new forms and the creative variability becomes exhausted relatively rapidly. Thus, the designer role goes beyond picking winners with every generation: he or she must be able to create novel abstract architectures or body-plans, and very few people if any know how to do that. In addition, if the designer is an architect or a structural engineer, there are other challenges to be met. The virtual forms in this case won't be merely aesthetic structures but must be structures *capable of bearing loads* (in compression, in tension etc).

Let me explain in more detail this important point. Some modern CAD systems already have a "history function" which keeps track of the steps needed to do solid modeling. Thus, if one creates a staircase or a column (or any other architectural component), the software keeps track of the sequence of operations which was used to generate such a component (a sequence of revolutions, extrusions and Boolean operations, for example). This sequence can, indeed, become the DNA for that particular virtual staircase or column. But unless some additional information is included, information defining the structural role that component will have (bearing loads in compression, for example, in the case of the column) as the virtual buildings begin to mate there will be nothing to constrain the components to a particular function. Columns may now evolve into useless cantilevers or staircases be turned upside down and placed in areas where they are meaningless functionally. In other words, the virtual building will not *evolve as a building*.

It is here that Deleuze and his philosophy of form will become necessary. As I said above, Deleuze sees singularities (phase transitions) as a key component of what the machinic phylum is. I gave one example, the simplest type, of these metamorphosing transitions: liquification or crystallization. But there are many others, such as the transition in a metal from magnetic to nonmagnetic, the transition in a flowing liquid from calm to turbulent, or the transition in the gait of a moving horse from trotting to galloping. In the study of real embryological development it has become clear that the embryo goes through an elaborate sequence of phase transitions, some of which divide the fertilized egg, others which change its symmetry from spherical to bilateral, others yet which mark the onset of the development of an arm or a finger. With each singularity crossed new traits of expression (to use Deleuze's term) emerge and become the stage for yet other phase transitions, each singularity adding complexity to the initially simple egg. Yet the egg itself, and its distribution of *intensive properties* (such as the intensity of concentration of certain chemicals) already has the capability to undergo those metamorphoses. The genes guide but do not command the final form. In other words, the genes do not contain a blueprint of the final form (a blueprint which would be an external form imposed on the egg) but tease out that final form from the egg by facilitating a phase transition here, inhibiting another one there, maneuvering the dynamic development process in certain directions and away from others.[11]

Architects and structural engineers will need to learn from real embryological processes, or to put it differently, they will have to become *egg designers*. In this case the distribution of intensive properties will not be one of chemical concentrations, but the *distribution of stresses* which any load bearing structure exhibits. In other words, in order for a building to evolve as a building, the columns (and the distribution of stresses produced by compressive forces) will have to be constrained to remain columns, unless other structural elements have evolved which change the stress distribution taking the load off the column and allowing it to become a decorative element evolving along purely aesthetic lines. And similarly for beams and other structural elements. The virtual evolutionary process will have to take place via phase transitions, with each singularity marking the emergence of a new structural element and a new distribution of stresses, and something within the software will have to ensure that the combination of structural elements remains coherent.

Clearly, performing all these tasks will involve going beyond the capabilities of most existing CAD programs. But when such a software is created (and I am sure that it will) the philosophy of form it will embody will be far away from that of the original CAD packages which worked with rigid polygons, the virtual version of obedient matter. Both the design of the software and the design of the eggs themselves will involve using know-how and skills to "track the machinic phylum", that is, to investigate the behavior of simulated evolution past certain singularities and the emergent wholes arising from the interactions between many components. It will also involve a cooperation between the designer and the virtual materials, a process where all parties have a say in the final form produced.

11 Brian Goodwin. *How the Leopard Changed its Spots*. (Simon & Schuster, New York 1996).Chapter 5.

Karl S.Chu > De Landa is a Deleuzean and as such a contemporary materialist who fervently reinterprets the behavior of the world in quasi-metallurgical terms.

A paradigm arises that is based on the convergence of information and biology. Life itself is information; we know this through the computer processing of DNA.

There are enough bits of evidence for understanding that everything is being absorbed by this universal form of information processing, which is evolutive, what's more. For that reason design processes become more genetic and evolutive, based on various types of evolutive platforms. Within this scenario, the authorship of architecture in its traditional sense finds itself weakened. In its place processes evolve that incorporate collective participation through working in cyberspace and in self-reproducing and self-organizing systems with a high degree of automatic autonomy.

A fundamental difference between Deleuze's position and computation is that Deleuze's philosophy is based on the metaphysics of continuity, taking for granted the logic of the infinitesimal founded on calculation within a still-classical notion of being. Computation necessitates a discrete logic of reality, based on quantum mechanics and logic. For this it's necessary to conceive design processes, among them architecture, from a combinatory information base in the form of bits.

Computation is a material process that consumes energy and not just abstract information. The paradigm proceeds from the idea of being as computation and as such suggests an ontology that is insufficient and incomplete when taking the logic and physical or energy limits of computation into consideration. We are still at the beginning of the development of genetic systems applicable to design processes, including architecture.

De Landa is absolutely right to argue that up to now a completely autonomous genetic system doesn't yet exist, one capable of generating morphologies appropriate to parameters that are sufficiently complex to be acceptable without a crucial contribution or intervention from outside. All this takes us no further than to a different vision of the world and of reality. We've only begun to scratch the surface of the tip of the iceberg, most of which is still invisible. For many people, even non-existent, alas.

Karl S. Chu is an experimental architect who has taught at the Sci Arch (Southern California Institute of Architecture) in Los Angeles since 1990. There he is nearer to the computer-design studios for cinema than to the conventional production of architecture. He is currently working on the development of a theoretical and practical base for architecture at the dawn of what he calls today's "infozoïc" age, in which the forms of artificial life proliferate and converge as an extension of nature as we know it.

synworld.t0.or.at/level3/symposium_neu/cam6.htm

Here begins the diary of a journey. Ljubljana in Slovenia, Graz in Austria and Zagreb in Croatia form a triangle of influences that define a particular identity, like a city of cities, beyond territorial limits. Sadar and Vuga, LOVE and njiric+njiric are three practices that represent – each at one of the vertices of the triangle – three similar yet at the same time different experiences in the social, cultural, economic or ideological contexts in which they are required to produce.

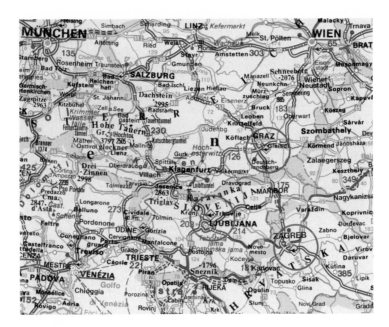

Welcome to central Europe,
where North meets South, and West meets East.

Ljubljana, December 1999. Dimičeva 13. Ten minutes
or so from the center, in an amorphous area in the
university and government district, there appears the
brightly lit green silhouette of the Slovenia Chamber of
Commerce and Industry. In 1991 Slovenia declared
itself independent. Jožko Čuk, president of the Chamber,
is one of the driving forces behind its modernization,
and also the most dogges defender of the scheme
Sadar Vuga Arhitekti presented to the competition for
the new headquarters.
Sadar was born in 1963 and Vuga in 1966.

further information in pages 208-219

Boštjan Vuga parks the car in an underground car park beneath the entrance plaza. Embedded in the carefully worked, pale marble paving of the plaza are lights and the inscription "dom gospodarstva". Soldiers from a nearby barracks pass opposite us. It's begun to snow. At either end of the building there are TV cameras. In no time at all the building has been nicknamed "Esmeralda", the main character in a Mexican soap opera that's very popular in Slovenia. People say, "Shall we meet in front of Esmeralda?"

We go up to the sixth floor, to the administrative offices.
Boštjan presents us to the public relations people. If we're in
a particular place, it's a place of transit. To us the building
looks increasingly like the embassy of a fast-moving nation
that doesn't exist but which has millions of inhabitants.
The neutral territory of a nation of airports, convention
centers, hotels, of high-tech consumerism, portable phones
and suitcases on wheels, of out-of-date fashions that are
fashionable once again, of exotic haute cuisine and excellent
wines, of computerized Pantone colors and textures.

We gradually work our way down the building via the vertical concourse. The office area is in fact smaller than before, but the amount of space intended for conference rooms, classrooms and other public areas has increased. On the third floor the librarian greets Boštjan effusively. She emphasizes how much her workspace has improved since the move to the new building. Opposite the library, the exhibition area is showing an installation; in the midst of the vertical void there's a green of artificial grass, with golf balls. Here, too, are the shoes of the presumed players who, between meetings, appear to have ended up making a birdie.

Every year, some 6,000 students pass through the three training centers in business management and other programs. The Chamber gives more than 120,000 consultations a year, mostly to small or medium-sized businesses. Apart from offering legal and commercial advice, it encourages the introduction of quality control, new technology and environmental protection.

The security personnel don't like the shape of the desk counter. It's easy to see why. They can't hide behind it, can't conceal their half-eaten sandwiches, and must keep their shoes well shined. But this is the Chamber of Commerce, you know. That's what Sadar and Vuga say. From the ground floor we look up.

It's started snowing again.

Leibnitz. Hasendorfstrasse 96. We're in the south of Austria. Landmark is the headquarters of two small companies who share the office fifty-fifty. By night the building, created by the team of architects from Graz, LOVE, gradually changes hue according to the four basic printing colors: cyan blue, magenta, yellow and green, in place of black. At first there was quite a lot of pressure from the local residents. Now they're grateful for the calming effect of this lighting in the middle of the night.

further information in pages 220-229

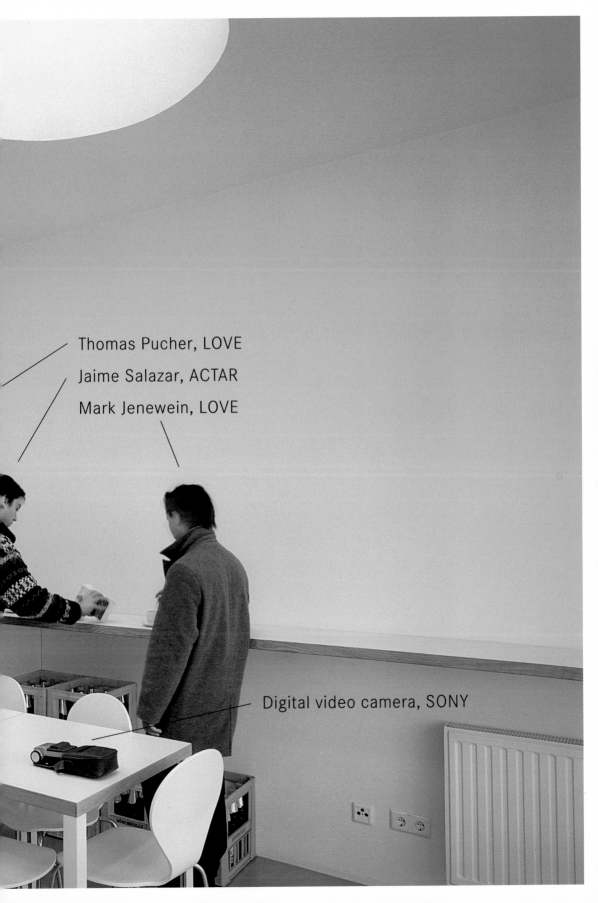

Thomas Pucher, LOVE

Jaime Salazar, ACTAR

Mark Jenewein, LOVE

Digital video camera, SONY

The building is raised two meters above the ground. It can be seen quite a way off in a landscape somewhere between rural and suburban. Barely a kilometer away there's a huge Baumaxx, the do-it-yourself and gardening hypermarket. The ramp connects the highway to the main entrance. It's reserved for customers, the employees park underneath the building.

Gerhard Agrinz, engineering consultants for crops and irrigation, and Joachim Schnedlitz, of Boom Software, share the building.

The two companies are somewhat different. They communicate with their clients, work and organize themselves in a different way. LOVE gets on better with Schnedlitz and his software company. Agrinz's engineering business is a bit more old-fashioned in its way of thinking and working. At least Schnedlitz has managed to install a computer network that works in Agrinz's office.

The climatic facade is a gallery running right around the building. It includes rest zones for smokers and non-smokers, meeting areas, balconies, two bathrooms and the entrance lobby. Each workstation gets three meters of gallery.
Three employees are smoking next to the kitchen.
Outside, there's quite a thick fog.

The two proprietors have a small private apartment, Schnedlitz's below, and Agrinz's above, the main office floor. Neither of these is used very much. Gerhard Agrinz regularly offers his clients and associates a tour of the building.

Judenberg. Hans-List-Strasse 6. One of the biggest communications groups in Austria sold a print shop to its workers, due to its bad siting and low volume of business.
A cooperative was formed and its manager, Bernd Payer, focused its activity on customer service and innovation.
The volume of business increased to the point that its facilities became too small. Payer got in touch with LOVE. Was it possible to build a new print shop twice the size of the old one and have a mortgage that cost less than the rent they were paying before?
Of course, LOVE replied.
The building cost € 603 per square meter.

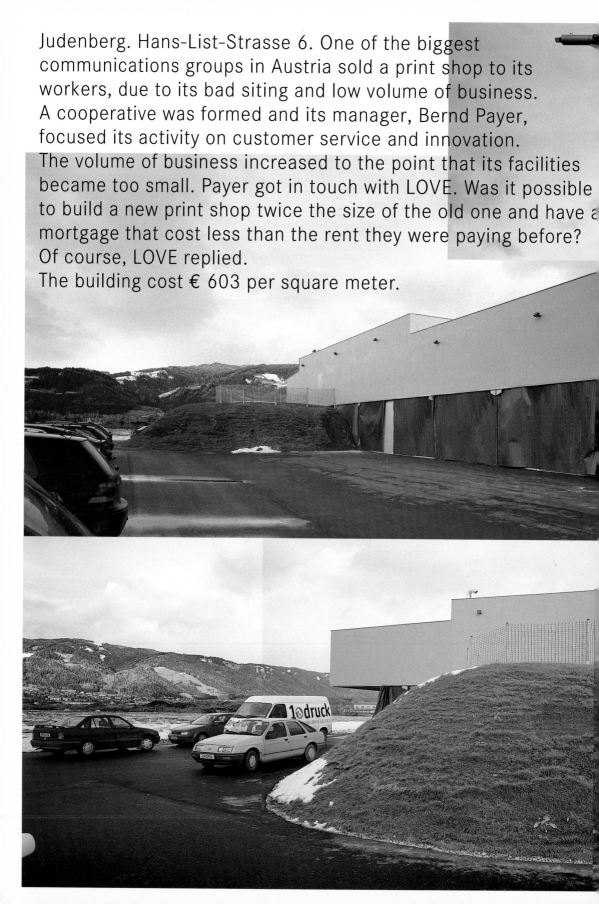

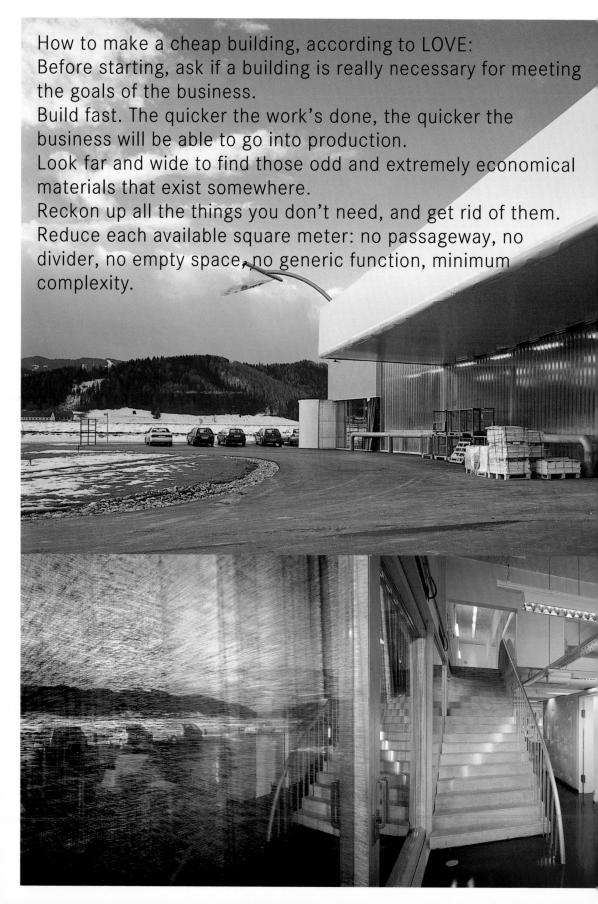

How to make a cheap building, according to LOVE:

Before starting, ask if a building is really necessary for meeting the goals of the business.

Build fast. The quicker the work's done, the quicker the business will be able to go into production.

Look far and wide to find those odd and extremely economical materials that exist somewhere.

Reckon up all the things you don't need, and get rid of them.

Reduce each available square meter: no passageway, no divider, no empty space, no generic function, minimum complexity.

Formulate an exact idea of what parts of the construction must have a refined finish, so that many more can stay rough. The parts with a rough finish must be built with greater quantities of material.
Make the clearest of contacts, and don't forget anything. Enter into long but sincere negotiations with the construction company. Be rigorous but fair in visits to the site.

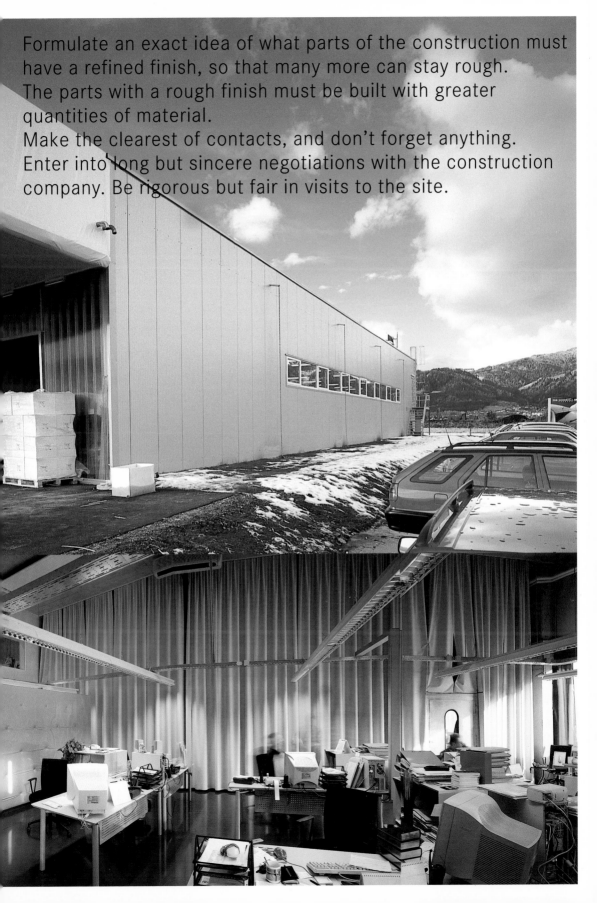

The next day, en route to Maribor, we visit the prototype mass-produced solar house that LOVE designed for Softech. This is the biggest of four pre-designed models, with their different sizes and configurations, built by the owner of the company to the south of Leibnitz, close to the frontier with Slovenia.
The interior of the house is laid out according to the criteria of feng-shui. We remove our shoes before entering.
It's a magnificent sunny winter morning.
www.softech.home.at

We arrive in Maribor. The suburbs either side of the entrance avenue are no different from any other town, but the Alpine mountains are very close. When night falls, the ski runs light up the white slopes. Between commercial buildings and low houses you find the atypical McDonald's drive-in restaurant by the team of Croatian architects, njiric+njiric.

We keep to this avenue for approximately a kilometer until reaching the other building constructed by njiric+ njiric, the Baumaxx do-it-yourself and gardening hypermarket. Just in front there's another McDonald's. Comparing this with the one njiric+njiric built, it's hard to understand how they managed to do it. It must be one of the only ones in the world that doesn't have the typical McDonald's look. Maybe because the big "M" is also bigger.

And so all the work created by Helena and Hrvoje is in this one kilometer, in a town in a neighboring country.

We eat a BigMac menu in the njiric+njiric McDonald's. There seems to be no alternative. Hrvoje greets the proprietor. This drive-in alone provides work for fifty people, he tells us later. The publicity handouts invite you to get into the franchise business. They're going to litter the whole country with drive-ins.

further information in pages 230-245

Baumaxx is a huge chain of do-it-yourself and gardening hypermarkets that since beginning in Austria is opening up in those countries of Eastern Europe nearest to the EEC, among them Slovenia, Croatia, Hungary, the Czech Republic and Slovakia. The Baumaxx aesthetic doesn't differ much from that of other major multinational chains, and in that sense the McDonald's and Baumaxx projects have something in common. The lit-up signs above the shopping center are so big they can be spotted from almost anywhere in the town.

Although technically, in the way they've been built, there aren't major differences between the njiric+njiric edifice and any other Baumaxx building, in each detail there's a latent desire to reconsider the usual technical and material practices by which these kinds of project are produced.

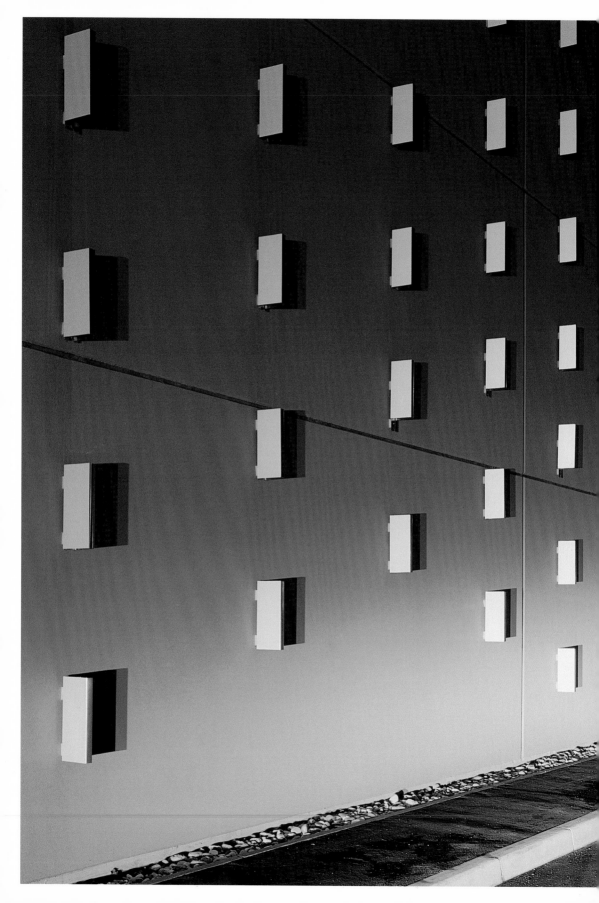

From everything, however conventional, it's possible to draw something magical. Even from a self-bearing concrete structure with huge windows, metal roof and concrete walls. That's why the walls are light up at night, like the slopes of the mountains nearby.

njiric+njiric also seek a more fluid relationship between architecture and the forms of consumerism in the information era. Yet their innovatory drive is met by a lack of understanding and, faced with the impossibility of building in their own country, they have to export their production. Between do-it-yourself (*bricolage*) and architects, is any relationship possible? As a structure of communication, *bricolage* works.
Bricolage can be more interactive than the vast majority of relationships between clients and architects.

The bosses of the hypermarket provide us with an extendible ladder, eight meters long, the longest they have on sale. We go up on the roof. It's a bit windy. Rain is threatening.

Unlike the lit-up signs, the artificial green roof goes unobserved by the inhabitants of Maribor. Helena and Hrvoje have transferred a bit of Slovenian countryside onto the conventional layout of a hypermarket, and from here it's difficult to know where you really are, if on the neighboring hills or in a typical suburban neighborhood. The only thing missing is Julie Andrews singing "The sound of Music" with her arms open wide.

9 : 00. microsoft-tehnično srečenj

9 : 00 priprava na zaključni raču

0 : 00 naddzorni svet-psuus

0 : 00 io-sekcije obrambne indust

odošli v gospodarski zbornici

slovenije

Ljubljana, 2000

The organization of space is an economic strategy, say Sadar and Vuga. And although basically it always has been, architecture, the creation of space, is not always associated with the desire to inject new energy into the system, which in the end is what defines any market, any living economy.

How should one respond from the stability of a built product to the dynamics of a global and computerized economy? For Sadar and Vuga, the evolution from the industrial towards the informational shows that the means of production no longer compete merely in their product/price ratio, but above all in their ability to adapt to the constantly growing and changing dynamics of the market.

If the dynamics of assimilation and consumption follow given schemes of logic, why not to try to adapt architectural production to these schemes? Fashion is one of them. And fashion is governed by certain periods, certain rhythms, certain communication strategies... which are also applicable – why not? – to the design and production of buildings. Only those cities – and those structures within cities – that develop mechanisms of motion in time and space are becoming centres of attraction for work and the generation of capital gains.

Sadar Vuga Arhitekti > January 1998. We finish our first publication which is at the same time our annual report, exhibition catalog and studio portfolio. Its concept is the result of intense cooperation between the editor, graphic designer, translator, and us. We want to present our work and the intensity of activity at the studio. At that time, we presume that 300 copies will be enough for presentations of the studio at home and abroad. The presumption is false: in September all we have left are samples for our archive.

Sadar Vuga Arhitekti have worked in strict collaboration with the London studio The Designers' Republic for some time now. The most recent fruit of this collaboration is the book *3D>2D*, published by Laurence King.

Welcome to the Chamber of Commerce and Industry of Slovenia

Already some time ago, we learned that modern work organization could not be achieved in the then existing premises. In the past, we had modernized the business premises of most regional chambers of commerce and industry. However, the premises in Ljubljana posed a very large problem, as its offices were spread among seven different locations. Consequently, communication and efficient work was significantly impaired. There was a lack of parking areas for clients in all locations, preventing large groups from meeting and employees from communicating with visitors. We also had problems with computers and communications as well as with providing space for different educational activities and in organizing conferences, seminars and business meetings at all levels.

The new building would provide the opportunity for the organizational modernization of the Chamber and the introduction of modern technology. All offices and services for companies would be organized at one location. The building could offer a functional venue for all manner of business meetings and there would be no more parking problems. Work would be simplified and rationalized, leading to greater efficiency and better service. The building would enable better communication between employees and clients. The office area would in fact be smaller than before, but with more conference rooms, classrooms and other public areas.

The new premises were constructed without additional burdening the members. It was performed within deadline, according to the financial plan and with local builders. Most materials and equipment are of Slovenian origin. Accordingly, the building will in itself be a special promotion of the country's economic potential.

Jožko Čuk, President, in *Chamber of Commerce and Industry of Slovenia, Ljubljana, 1999*
Gospodarska zbornica Slovenije — Chamber of Commerce and Industry of Slovenia
Dimičeva 13, SI-1000 Ljubljana.
www.gzs.si

> VERB

For the design of the Chamber of Commerce, Sadar and Vuga had the complicity of their clients, especially of its chairman, Jožko Čuk. Slovenia is young and small, but wide awake. The Chamber of Commerce is its metaphor: an open context, defined by a strong desire to integrate and compete within a global panorama. The Chamber of Commerce is a megastore that stimulates the flow of variable capital and thus generates new fields of investment in this part of the world.

CHAMBER OF COMMERCE AND INDUSTRY OF SLOVENIA. Dimičeva 13, Ljubljana
Site area: 4,640 sqm. Building area: 1,194 sqm. Total floor area: 18,189 sqm. Client: Chamber of Commerce and Industry of Slovenia. Competition design: Jurij Sadar, Boštjan Vuga, Špela Videčnik, Tadej Zaucer. Design: Jurij Sadar, Boštjan Vuga, Jurij Sadar Sr., Tadej Zaucer, Josip Konstantinovic, Aljosa Dekleva, Simona Muc, Anton Zizek, Tatjana Kercmar, Peter Senk. Structural engineering: Elea (Angelo Zigon, Andrej Pogacnik). Service engineering: Biro ES. Landscape: Ana Kucan. Signage: studioBotas. Lighting: Studio Japelj. Art works: Alan Ozbolt, Zora Stancic, Petra Varl. Photographs: Igor Omahen, Jože Suhadolnik, Ramon Prat.

THE PROJECT IN A DIAGRAM...

"The diagram represents Sadar and Vuga arhitekti's project approach. If there is no product, there is no communication amongst the individual links in the process. If there is a disturbance or if the communication between the links is disrupted, the effect of the architectural product changes. Therefore: if we want to accomplish the desired effect, we must control the communication between client, project group and the public during the evolution of the design." From their résumé of the studio's activity in the year 1998.

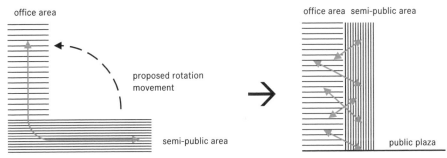

Traditional diagram of an administrative building.
Hierarchical and lineal relationships between uses.

Chamber of Commerce and Industry of Slovenia.
Compacity and multiple interrelation between spaces.

THE RESULTING SPATIAL ORGANIZATION...

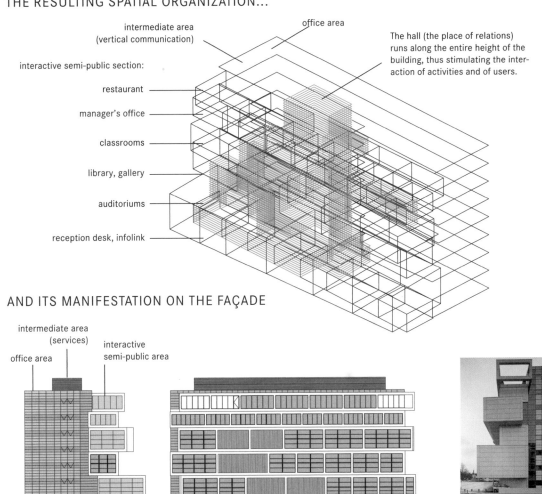

intermediate area
(vertical communication)

office area

interactive semi-public section:

restaurant

manager's office

classrooms

library, gallery

auditoriums

reception desk, infolink

The hall (the place of relations) runs along the entire height of the building, thus stimulating the inter-action of activities and of users.

AND ITS MANIFESTATION ON THE FAÇADE

intermediate area
(services)

office area

interactive
semi-public area

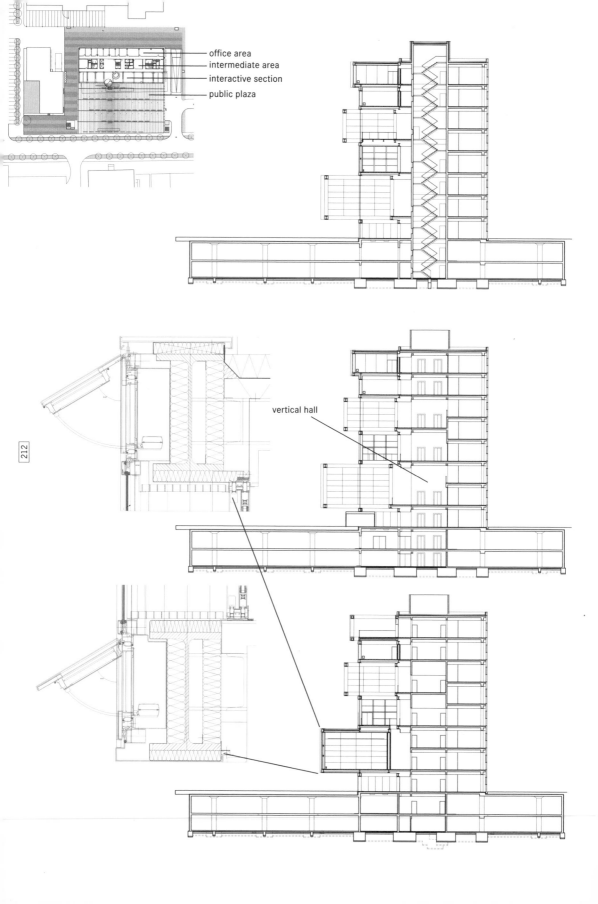

office area
intermediate area
interactive section
public plaza

vertical hall

offices +7

11%
vertical hall

restaurant,
banquet hall

offices +6

7%
vertical hall

manager's office

offices +5

23%
vertical hall

classrooms

offices +4

6%
vertical hall

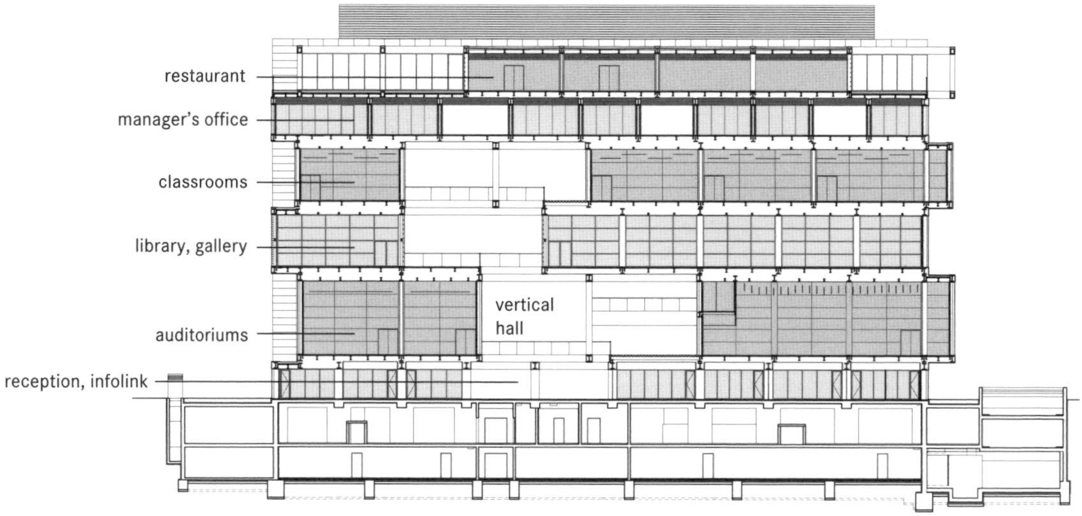

restaurant

manager's office

classrooms

library, gallery

auditoriums

vertical
hall

reception, infolink

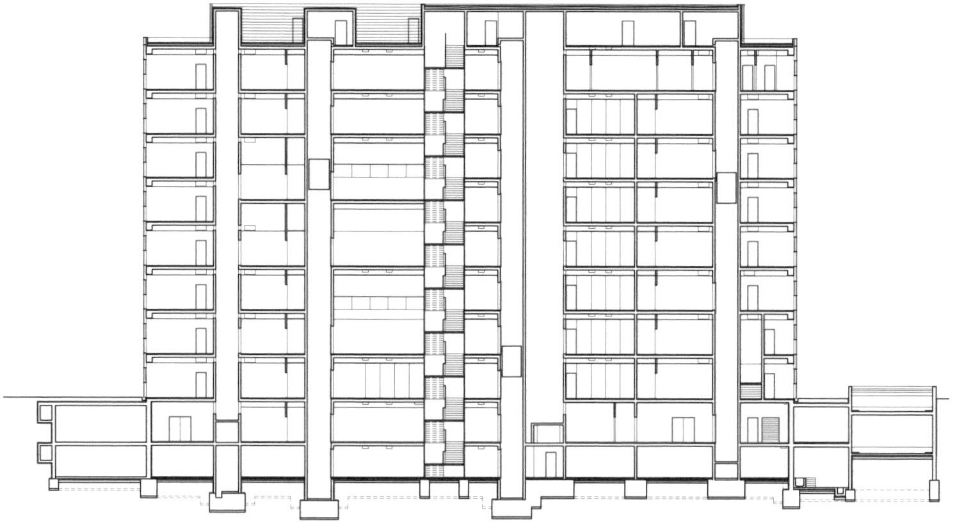

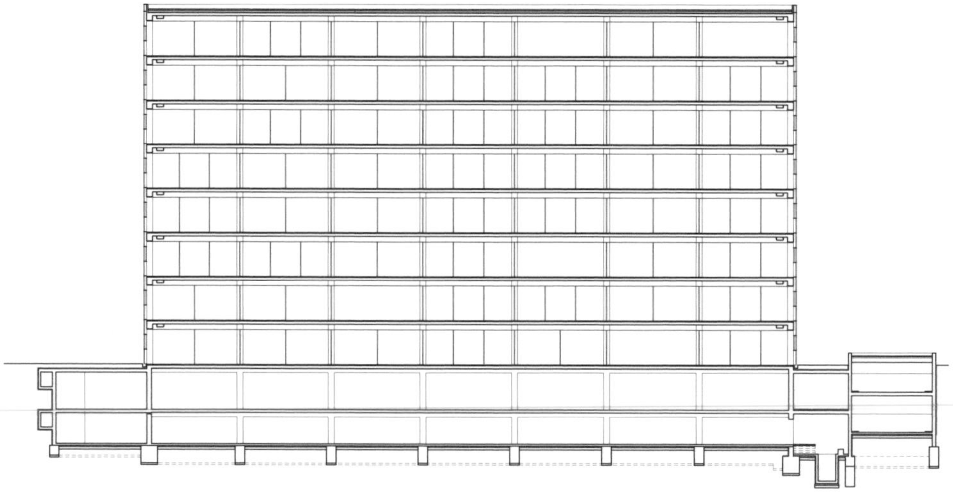

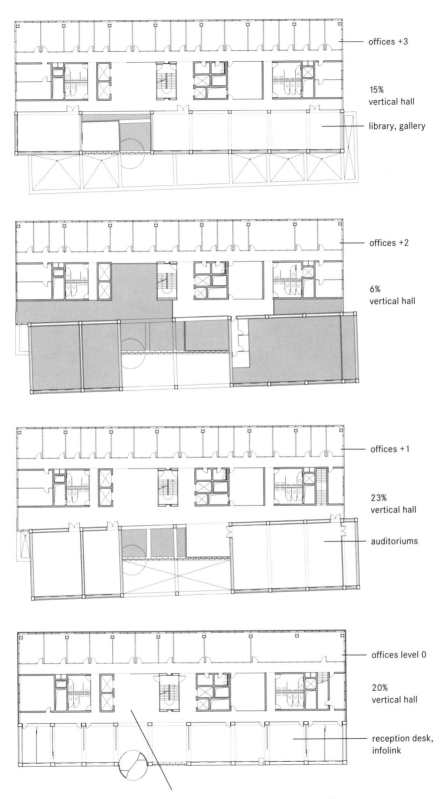

offices +3

15%
vertical hall

library, gallery

offices +2

6%
vertical hall

offices +1

23%
vertical hall

auditoriums

offices level 0

20%
vertical hall

reception desk,
infolink

The vertical hall is the place for meeting, waiting,
viewing and rest. It is a communicative space which
stimulates the intensity of the institution.

Office diary

01.98 > Exhibition 4+1, four competitions and one commission. For the first time, we present ourselves to the widest public. Most of all, we make our presence known. How we work, communicate, what kind of service someone who comes to us can expect and what she or he can get in a certain phase of project development. We don't exhibit in a gallery, but rather in the lobby of an office building. The fluctuation is greater, as well as the communication between the people and the exhibited objects, the foreseen effect is greater.

02.98 > Interior design. The building proceeds as planned. There are difficulties in coordinating the services in the first basement. The walls are built, and about two hundred cavities of various sizes are not there. Whose fault is it? The architects'? The structural engineer's? The service engineer's? Lots of noise, the investor puts a halt to our payments, then all is suddenly quiet. A sort of artificial panic. Noise at the studio as well. We are literally under siege by various subcontractors for the building. The studio is overflowing with samples of textile floors, parts of partition walls, catalogs of office furniture. We then introduce a price list of consulting fees. We notify the salesmen by phone when they inquire about the conditions, and the number of offers significantly diminishes.

03.98 > Interior design deadline. We introduce ourselves at the festival Sarajevska zima – Sarajevo Winter – with the same exhibition that we held in Ljubljana in January. This time in collaboration with studioBotas design studio, which designs a poster, a graphic and iconographic interpretation of the exhibit. We intend the poster to be an associative announcement of the project that does not communicate with the public via architectural techniques but rather with the language of advertising, of street posters. It is a visual piece of information, an ad for a certain project. What do we expect from a presentation in Sarajevo? It is the first step onto a new market, that will offer possibilities for work. There is much to be built. Nothing for now. But we have been to Sarajevo.

04.98 > All concrete walls in the interior are designed in exposed concrete, with no particular finishing. The subcontractor that was responsible for the walls did not execute them to a standard that would allow the walls to remain exposed (béton brut). There is more than one reason: the subcontractor works at very short deadlines, meaning that many walls are descaffolded too soon; there are difficulties in coordinating the work with the subcontractors for the services, meaning that cavities and canals for the services are being drilled later. And, finally, we have not drawn the elevations of the walls, with all the hollows and electrical outlets. We are pressed for time. Conclusion: we now know that the concrete will be coated with paint. At the same time, we can claim that the building and the shape that it is taking are the result of an educated, liberal and courageous client's trust in the architects.

05.98 > How much time can we afford to spend preparing a relatively demanding competition project? We estimate that two project assistants can prepare a conceptually resolved project in three weeks. We require two weeks to establish a project group and concept, so the competition project is in the studio for at least five weeks. Each competition is an investment for the studio. It is financed by other projects. At the same time, winning a competition is a foundation for new work, and thus profit. Competitions are risks. If you try to be inventive, the risk is so much greater. But, if you do take the risk, you take it to the extreme. In order to develop and present an inventive project, you need more time, which increases the cost of the studio. Therefore, operationally speaking, we have to win competitions.

06.98 > Construction continued.

07.98 > Press conference. There is a short celebration in front of the building. The rough construction work is over. The concrete part has eight stories; the steel part consists of six boxes, set one on top of another. The secondary structure seems too strong, but it won't be visible in the end. We are glad that the whole thing looks like a magnified model. Two buildings, concrete and steel, stuck together. There are no major differences from project to execution. The effect in this phase still resembles the design. The President of the Chamber of Commerce and Economy holds the first press conference about the functioning of the Chamber in the future great hall. Because everything is open, the projection is invisible due to the sunlight. But it is comfortably cool.
It is summer. We are active on three construction sites. The functioning of the studio is not adapted to constant calls from subcontractors and the supervising engineer, constant corrections and unplanned meetings. All this drastically alters the pulse at the studio and our regular brainstorming sessions. With all the work and the number of people at the studio, we have no more resources. Besides that, it's vacation time. The attic in the studio has no air conditioning. Outside, the summer is long and hot. In short, hectic.

08.98 > Press conference. We are doing two projects that are not crucial for the studio – the bridge on the river Mura and the Moretti-Saranovic house. The first is a competition project for which we could have supposed that we had no realistic chances of winning despite a good solution. The second is commissioned by a nice and charming lady. From the very beginning, the commission shows signs of difficulty in transforming from utopia to reality. The projects cause financial loss and loss of time. For the first time in two years, the syntagm "project selection" appears.

09.98 > Why do we cultivate public relations? Why do we issue a press release every other month? We don't deny self-promotion, but our main goal is the demystification of our activities. We want to encourage communication among architects, between architects and clients as well as between architects and the public. We want to influence the architectural environment and shape it with our work. We want our activity to affect society. This is the spirit of the brochure that is to be published for the opening of the Chamber of Commerce and Economy building. We invite five world-renowned authors and a photographer – their texts should make the public conscious of the building. Thus, these authors become part of the project group, since the final effect of the building should to a great extent depend on their opinions. That is the scenario, what we need to do is establish the financial means and find an editor.

10.98 > Two things happen: we get our first big commission, a commercial-residential complex, and our first invitation to a competition – for the renovation of the assembly hall of the Slovenian parliament. Does this mean that we can earn the trust of clients and competition committees even though we haven't finished a single building? Of course neither fact should influence our approach to architecture design or the quality of presentation. A step in the evolution of the studio.

11.98 > This is the month that we turn down a project for the first time. Also due to the fact that we are not big enough to carry it out the way we want. A project assistant who has been with us from the start leaves the studio. Even if the production is ample enough, the internal structure of the ten employees is a little shaky. Time for changes: no more equality. How to establish a system of delegating and assessing the value of the work? There is no way to evaluate the input by hour, as what we do is integrated design. Next step in our evolution.

12.98 > The building now has its own, almost final outer image. The boxes in hygienic green, stacked one on top of another that together form the front are almost surreal on a gray winter day. The building is like a model in 1:1.

01.99 > Furnishing inside. Offices-complaints of the client's technical experts that sound insulation of the partitioning is not sufficient. It means that a subcontractor had to remove all walls and fill them with glass wool, which brought substantial chaos to the communication between supervision and the contractor. Vertical hall and circulation areas – we almost couldn't believe it – just looks as it should. Semi-public, box interiors – the uppermost part of all interiors – are not satisfactory due to the client's choice of a more reasonably priced subcontractor not turning out good. Edge to edge joint, what seems to be the easiest way certainly isn't. We are counting failures hoping that we are the only ones who will ever notice them.

02.99 > Our product of the month is for sure the reception desk. It is a freestanding yellow object. The form is computer-generated on the basis of a Moebius Strip. We experienced a beauty of transaction (and all troubles, of course) of a complex surface screen coordinates into 1:1 scale. What seems highly sophisticated as a design process, turns out to be almost primitive as a construction technique. Steel ribs are bent in order to ensure structure stability and form, then everything is wrapped with adhesive tape and then fiberglass is moulded around. Similar to boat manufacturing. The desk is punctuated by thin cables which connect five points on the ground with five points of the main steel structure above. One cannot really figure out whether the desk stands on the ground or is hanging from above. The desk floats. Of course, we would have never predicted that the form of the desk would almost make access to the building for us impossible. Security guys don't like it. It's obvious: they cannot hide behind it, cannot hide half-eaten sandwiches and they must have clean shoes. But this is the Chamber of Commerce.

03.99 > Moving in. Two hundred and twenty employees can't get used to a new space so easily. It's drafty; the air-conditioning is too strong, they claim that they are getting colds and flu. It's not comfortable. (A month later everything seems to be OK, although the air-conditioning is regulated at the same level as the month before.) But we are happy, since the employees' complaints are minor.

We prepared an operator's manual on how to make most of the CCIS architectural effects. 26 March is the inauguration day. We claim that the building is a result of an unusually good communication between client, design team, supervision and contractors.

04.99 > The CCIS building is nicknamed Esmeralda, after the heroine of a Mexican soap opera, extremely popular in Slovenia. So it is accepted positively by the public as well. "Should we meet in front of Esmeralda?" they say.

05.99 > First phase of the domestication of the building: vegetation in Tuscan-style pots spreads out over the corridors without us being asked. Shall we complain or is it simply too late?

06.99 > The president ordered the refurbishing of his office and a salon to another architect. When works are done and after he is re-elected we go to congratulate him. When asked what we think about the new look of the room, we honestly say that it very much fits with the building.

The end

architecture and urbanism

LOVE
Hans Sachsgasse 8/2
A-8010 Graz
November 1988

Hello LOVE,

Your company's printed stationery is now taking shape. Finally (for me too) there's a product that can function as a brand. Your "product" is great, it's attractive and it works. You should show it and let it appear like that with no problem at all, and what's more the name LOVE works perfectly OK as a brand name. I'm convinced that this is the right way to good communication, and that's exactly what the design of the stationery has to show and what it must try and represent. The graphics and the images have to be attractive and honest; the design touch mustn't show through, because you amply fulfil this yourselves.

Whoever collaborates with you should be able to come up with a specific image of LOVE via your visiting cards, letter paper or envelopes. The photos and drawings must never give the feeling of being publicity oriented, they must be manifestly part of a whole and not be too defined. Your image must be clear-cut and open-ended. I think that catalogue-wise, a folder system with detachable sheets is better for you than a luxury book. We ought to look for a system together that's pleasant, individual and also somehow interactive.

Best wishes

Letter written by Zündel, from the graphic design agency for LOVE

Graz, in southern Austria, is the city of the seven members of LOVE. They know that one possible approach to production goes beyond aesthetic debate and architecture competitions. Too much time lost winning second prizes. Is that the only way to try to produce quality architecture? How do you get a particular product to the client who really needs it?

One day, LOVE stopped reading architecture and started follow marketing courses. They themselves say that they've got more out of it than out of years of theories. Naturally, it's not the solution for everybody. One small comment by way of explanation: they were already good before they went over to economics.

LOVE BRAND

"Tommy Hilfiger knows: in a (very) crowded marketplace branding is more important than ever. It is the age of the brand! Anything can be branded (e.g. milk, chicken). Branding is as much for the very wee outfit as for Levi's, Nike, Starbucks or Intel (Inside)." Tom Peters

Brands communicate, stand for a special, unmistakable image and long-term thinking.
LOVE is a brand, because LOVE communicates a specific image.
Image and brand together explain what the customer can expect from LOVE:
— they serve to clearly position our company, our service and our products on the market
— they clearly define our products in the marketplace
— they bind customers to our company emotionally
and above all: brands can be used for marketing

LOVE MARKETING

Generally speaking, architects are faced with the problem of "selling" their services. Every business, every production facility, every private individual and all public institutions and organisations are actually potential customers – but they may not ever become "real" customers.

The "classic" marketing channel for young architects is always considered to be public competitions. We have not won a single competition. Nor do we see any point in investing an average 500 (unpaid) hours in competing against 300 colleagues in the hope of winning.

There are good reasons why the magic word of the last few years has been marketing. It provides answers to key questions such as:

Why should someone buy something from LOVE?
Why should someone build with LOVE?
How can we be better than our competitors?
What surplus value does the customer obtain through us?
What are our basic/core abilities, what are our USP's?

To answer these questions, it is essential to
— do benchmarking, i.e. to analyse the success of other companies from other branches and to use them as terms of reference,
— to precisely define and delimit target groups (customers)
— to study trends of the future (primarily social trends, followed by architectural trends)

LOVE's strategic goal for the future is therefore the development of products:
Target-group oriented solutions devised for specific needs, which can then be offered specifically on the market and to the target groups in question.

Landmark

START: The owners of two companies from different lines of business (= different visions, goals, strategies, customers) meet in the garden of a café in a very small town in southern Austria. Each of them plans to build and spontaneously they decide to build a joint office building to provide space for their expanding companies, to present themselves and to benefit from mutual synergetic effects.

COMPETITION: Whereas one of the two investors already conducts preliminary talks with LOVE, the other requires further information before deciding on his choice of architect. A competition is held and four architecture offices are invited to submit proposals. LOVE wins the competition for the following reasons:
1. We asked the most questions (systematic questioning technique)
2. We listened carefully
3. We found out what was really needed
4. We presented a concept consisting of ideas and possibilities, not a design

JOB SPECIFICATION: Planning and realising a building works like an independent company, which is formed following initial talks with the investor and systematically scaled down once the building is handed over. In order to ensure that the project is realised without hitches, the following points have to be clarified before any consideration at all can be given to design.
1. What is the corporate objective?
2. What strategy does the company pursue in order to achieve this objective?
3. What role does the building play in this strategy?
4. What requirements must the building therefore fulfil?
5. What minimum criteria must be met for the project to be successful?

LANDMARK. Hasendorferstrasse 96. Leibnitz (Austria)
Clients: Gerhard Agrinz Engineering, Boom software. Architects: L.O.V.E. architecture and urbanism. Light concept: fn systems, Flora Neuwirth. Builder: Thierbau GmbH (Unterpremstätten). Roofing: Hagen (Leibnitz). Locks: Lepold (Graz). Floors: Kah (Graz). Dry-assembly Construction: Ruckenstuhl (Leibnitz). Painting: Bscheider (Unterpremstätten). Exterior walls: Golds (Michlgleinz). Electricity: Scherbinek GmbH & Co KG (Unterpremstätten). Engineering: Kindermann GmbH (Leibnitz). Interiors: Breitenthaler (Gralla). Photographs: Andreas Ballon, Steffen Strassnig, Ramon Prat.

Ing. Gerhard Agrinz
Engineering consultants for crops and irrigation

Mr. Joachim Schnedlitz
BOOM software corporation

Providing answers to these questions leads to the actual needs which the project must fulfil. These are described precisely as job specifications (communication, personal needs) or expressed in figures (function, sales, size, costs, time).

The job specifications form the basis of the project and are signed by all those involved.

DESIGN: The design of the building is a direct response to the job requirements. The quality of the design increases in line with the diversity of requirements, the way that they can be meaningfully combined and our creative abilities.

WHY DOES IT LOOK THE WAY IT LOOKS?: landmark is the headquarters of two very different companies. Each operates in a different way, communicates with its customers in a different way, organises its work differently, has different visions and a different self-image.

And despite all this, they are supposed to share a building.

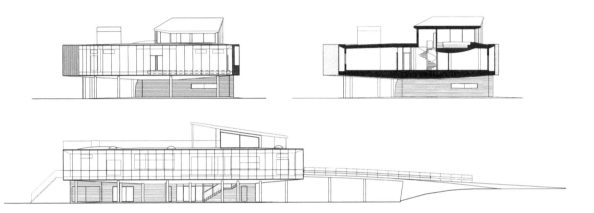

Landmark essentially consists of a ring on supports with downward and upward extensions. A number of factors were decisive for choosing this concept.

VISIBILITY: Requirement: signage. The building lies on a busy main road. The road is two metres higher than the level of the site of the building. In other words, the building has to be higher in order to be seen.

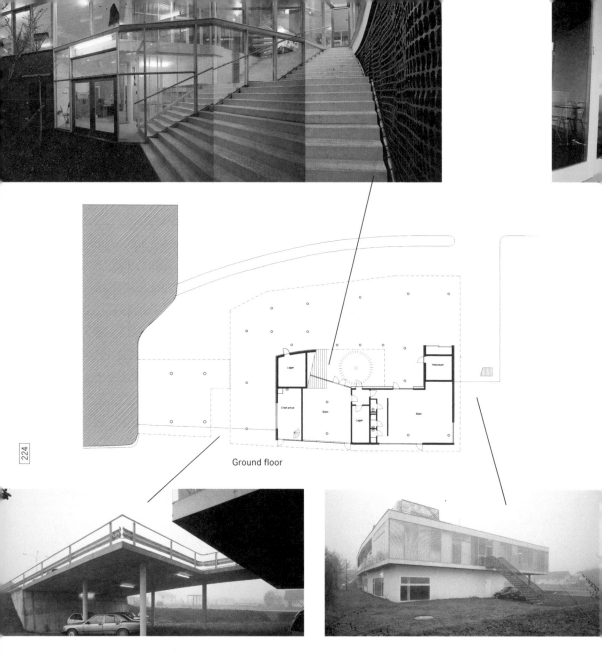

Ground floor

POTENTIAL FOR EXTENSION: Each company has different plans for expansion.

<u>Requirement</u>: rapid growth by expansion and consolidation of the existing location and formation of regional offices. In other words, landmark can be extended linearly by 300% for one company, whereas the ground floor can (if necessary) be extended for the other company.

A broad ramp links the main road and the main entrance. Access to this ramp is exclusively reserved for the customers of the two companies (parking for employees is located beneath the building). The ramp is on a slight incline and the approach to the entrance is reminiscent of an airport. <u>Requirement</u>: prestige.

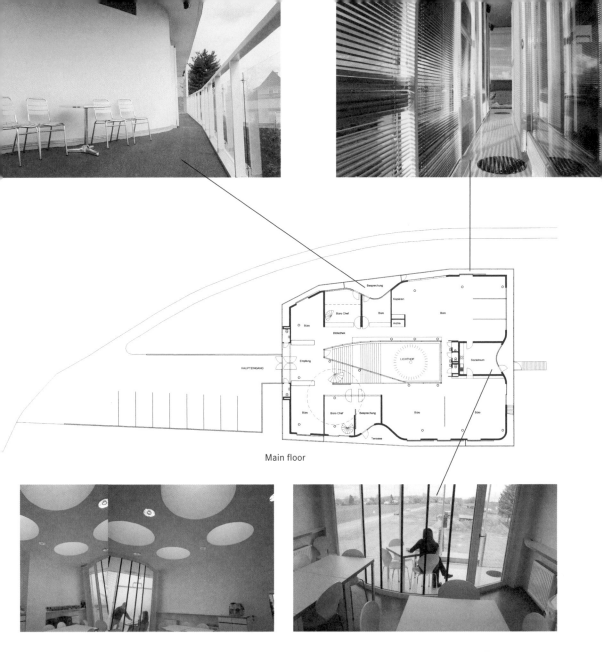

Main floor

Requirement: personal freedom. Neither of the employees of either company has any direct financial stake in the company. In other words they do not own the building. This means that open space constitutes areas which are unequivocally free, i.e. can be used as personal property. Open space is arranged in two layers around the core zone of the building.

1. The climate facade in the form of a full-scale wintergarden surrounds the entirety of the building. It contains areas for breaks (smoking and non-smoking), conference rooms, terraces, access to the roof, two WCs, the main entrance, noise protection, lighting control. There are 3 square metres of wintergarden for each workplace.

2. Outside space (garden, roof, terrace) is equipped with a computer hook-up at least every 25 metres. A substantial proportion of work is done outside during the summer months.

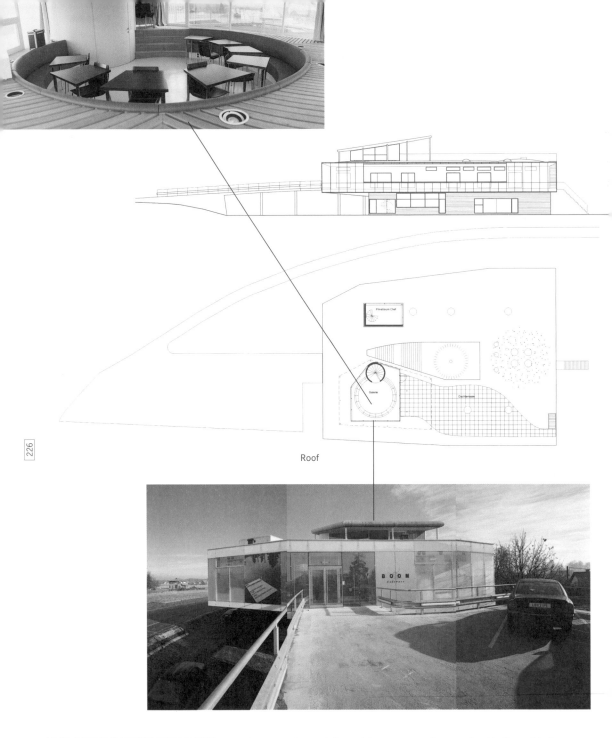

Roof

THE CORE OF THE BUILDING. <u>Requirement</u>: the workflow of the core zone is organised in line with the corporate structures of the two companies. Executive offices and conference rooms are located in the centre of each company and are the only self-contained/private/confidential areas; at the same time they separate the surrounding space into working areas of different, practical sizes (communication versus noise nuisance).

The supporting zones directly adjoin the core area. The seminar room in the loft, hardware on the ground floor, café and fresh air in the middle.

CLIMATE. The building is kept cool using natural means. <u>Requirement</u>: energy. The climate facade has ventilation openings in the floors and ceilings regulated by thermostats. Due to the incidence of sunlight in the summer there is an upward vertical current of air of several metres per second (chimney effect). If the windows to the inner courtyard and the climate facade are opened, the climate facade sucks the cool, still air from the inner courtyard through the office areas. These remain pleasantly cool.

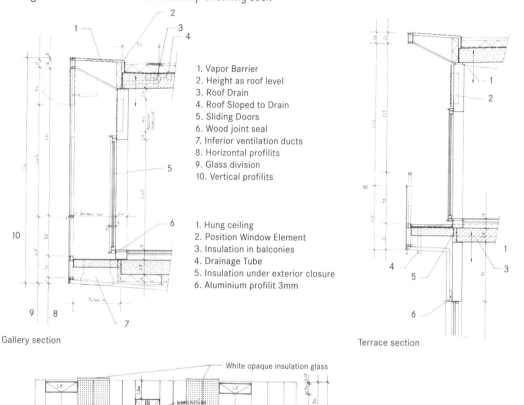

1. Vapor Barrier
2. Height as roof level
3. Roof Drain
4. Roof Sloped to Drain
5. Sliding Doors
6. Wood joint seal
7. Inferior ventilation ducts
8. Horizontal profilits
9. Glass division
10. Vertical profilits

1. Hung ceiling
2. Position Window Element
3. Insulation in balconies
4. Drainage Tube
5. Insulation under exterior closure
6. Aluminium profilit 3mm

Gallery section

Terrace section

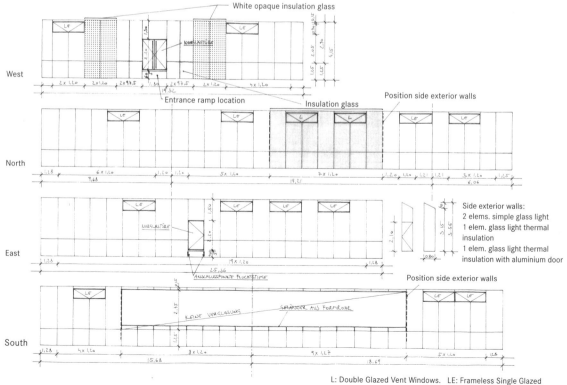

White opaque insulation glass

West

Entrance ramp location

Position side exterior walls

Insulation glass

North

Side exterior walls:
2 elems. simple glass light
1 elem. glass light thermal insulation
1 elem. glass light thermal insulation with aluminium door

East

Position side exterior walls

South

L: Double Glazed Vent Windows.   LE: Frameless Single Glazed

PLANNING. Planning is the minimum requirement in terms of time and means in order to achieve the goal of the project. LOVE carries out planning as "guideline planning", i.e. where it is indispensable, planning is very detailed and precise, but where it is not essential it allows the companies a certain amount of discretion. This approach leads to substantial savings in terms of costs and time, but also necessitates unequivocal contractual agreements and precise building management.

BUILDING. We envisage realisation through a general contractor for all our buildings, i.e. the building contract is awarded to one company, which distributes individual kinds of work to sub-contractors and itself acts as construction manager. The general contractor assumes responsibility for ensuring that all building work is carried out properly. The advantages for the investor are self-evident:
one contractual partner only = one (fully) liable partner = reduced project time = high degree of guaranteed costs
What this means for LOVE is that the general contractor in project management has to be meticulously checked and given every support from the very beginning. This can be achieved by the following means:

quality: building site protocol with the nature of a contract, weekly
          checklist, outstanding points, deadlines, weekly
          who is responsible for what, precise allocation of responsibilities, at the beginning of the project
costs: costs schedule, price increases and reductions, weekly
time: time schedule, structured according to building sections, weekly update

LANDMARK BUILDING PROCESS:

time		
preliminary talks	3	months
competition	2	days
negotiations on fees	5	weeks
analysis of needs	3	weeks
design (architecture)	10	weeks
design (detailed planning and schedule of work and services)	4	weeks
permission from public authorities	5	weeks
sending of offer	3	weeks
negotiations with bidders (construction companies)	10	weeks
drawing up contracts with construction companies	1	week
construction period	7	months
installation of fittings	2	weeks
post-construction services	12	months

REACTION. Mr. Schnedlitz had a comprehensive analysis of his office carried out. All internal areas and their surroundings were evaluated: the building scored the highest number of points in all areas.
Mr. Agrinz regularly invites customers and partners to tours of the building. The Steiermark Chamber of Commerce has invited itself to hold its next general meeting in the conference room in the loft.
Neighbours thanked the investors for the "soothing effect" of the lighting at night.
The wintergarden and the social room are always used by at least two people.
The banker responsible for arranging financing of the projects lives in a LOVE apartment.
Following initial difficulties, the companies carrying out construction work came to be real partners. Further joint projects are already in progress.
Traditional architecture magazines are not interested in publishing anything on such projects.
Verb was very enthusiastic, but it took almost two years to publish it.
LOVE has learnt a great deal and is very satisfied with the result.

At night slowly changing phases illuminate Landmark in the four primary colours used in printing – yellow, blue, green and magenta. <u>Requirement</u>: pleasure. The concept was devised by the artist Flora Neuwirth. <u>Requirement</u>: prestige. We often collaborate with Flora Neuwirth. <u>Requirement</u>: new ideas.

Flora Neuwirth > My conception of what is optimal in art and building is collaboration between architects, artists and users from the very beginning of the planning stage. As this is not possible in the case of every project, I try to create interaction by means of intervention.

It is conceivable that the project in the Landmark office is reminiscent of the Spaceship Enterprise, an installation by James Turrell or that the building itself brings an American bar to mind and the terrace evokes a feeling of a fifties sanatorium. However, this is not an arbitrary decision, but is based on my interest in combining contents and aesthetic perceptions from different times and sources and integrating art and architecture, popular culture, advertising and daily life in projects.

In contrast to the office areas, the facade is not defined spatially. For me it constitutes the interface between the inside (office space) and outside (open space) of the building. The 'illusion of an additional dimension' in this area is intended to create a zone which is undefined and permits subjective perception.

Areas of colour on the walls are, on the one hand, intended to create restful places for workers in this area, and, on the other hand, the stuck-on advertising slogans – whereby the product is replaced by colour – are intended to create a reference to outside space. Yellow and pink dominate the north side of the building, cyan and green the south side. The spatial atmosphere is defined by the balance between warm and cold tones.

Over the last few years Flora Neuwirth has developed a universally applicable system which can be used under the label fnsystems© for a wide range of design areas, related to the art context as well as to design and popular culture.

design a dream with yellow
sweet pink for a daily balance
pop up with blue
keep in shape with blue
chill out on green

The end

1A Druck

START. The 1a druck printing company was bought by its employees three years ago. The parent company, one of the largest media groups in Austria, sold the business on account of its peripheral location and low volume of sales. The new company of owners, represented by its managing director, Mr. Payer, focussed on the core competence of the business: customer service and innovation.

Sales rose exponentially and after only two years the existing building was too small to accommodate the planned new machinery. This was when Mr. Payer contacted LOVE.

The challenge was to construct a new building which was 50% larger than the existing one at a cost which was so low that repayment instalments of the loan taken out to finance the building would be lower than the rent of the existing building.

THE REQUIREMENTS. A further analysis of the company revealed the following requirements:
1. price/sqm < € 726
2. utmost flexibility: use of the building was to have the same degree of flexibility as that of an empty carpark
3. growth: when fully operational, the building will have the capacity of growing by up to 500%
4. fun: The building itself does not have to be funny, but it is to be a fun place to work.

THE DESIGN. The Las Vegas concept. The building is located on a corner lot, directly at the entrance to a large industrial estate. The south and west sides lie along the access roads (prominent view; the north and east sides are typical rear sides (out of sight).

To keep construction costs as low as possible, our design of the building followed the Las Vegas principle: all attention to the front, nothing but the cheapest in the back.

However, the design of the front sides does not follow Las Vegas principles (a printing company is not a hotel). Its attributes are not those of prestige and flashiness but rather those associated with user-friendliness. A grassy hill as an observation point, the entrance through a corner stone, the delivery zone as a typical forecourt, curtains walls in front of a luxury glass facade, above a wall in seventies-style glitter look.

PRINTING COMPANY 1A DRUCK. Hans-List-Straße 6. Judenburg, Austria
Client: Aichfelder Druckerei S.A. Architects: L.O.V.E. architecture & urbanism, Thomas Pucher (technical project), Mark Jenewein (organization), Peter Kilian (supervising). General contractor: Zaunfuchs Bau (Judenburg). Structural engineering, metal structures: Profilstahl S.A.(Judenburg). Painting: W. Poharec (Judenburg). Flat roof waterproofing: Fleischmann & Petschnig (Neumarkt). Wood: F. Golds (Michlgleinz). Electricity: Moder Elektrotechnik (Judenburg). Engineering: Hopf S.A. (Knittelfeld). Photographs: Ramon Prat

LOFT + FUNCTION + FLEXIBILITY + CONNECTION + COMMUNICATION

The fundamental spatial requirement was very simple: a hall in which there is a place for everything and everything is in its place. Were it not for the fact that the printing presses produce noise, heat and humidity, the walls within the hall would not have been necessary. Functional processes in the building formed the central pattern on which the ground plan is organised. Supplies of paper are delivered in the south-east and stored in the rear area of the hall beside the printing presses (offsetting differences in temperature). Customers arrive at the office in the south-west, where the order is then passed on to the pre-printing stage (behind the "cushion area"), where graphics are done and then to the exposure area where the printing plates are prepared (at the very back). The plates then go directly to the printing-works and are inserted into the printing presses from the front while the paper is fed in from the back. Once the printing process is completed, the piles of paper are transported through the centre of the hall in a southerly direction to the binding section and from there – in large batches – for dispatch (= delivery) in the south-east or – as small batches – to the front office in the south-west, where they can be collected directly. All work stations are linked with each other by a direct line of communication.

PROCESS

preliminary talks	3	months
negotiations on fees	3	days
analysis of needs	5	weeks
design (architecture)	8	weeks
design (detailed planning and schedule of work and services)	4	weeks
permission from public authorities	5	weeks
sending of offer	3	weeks
negotiations with bidders (construction companies)	6	weeks
drawing up contracts with construction companies	3	weeks
construction period	5	months
installation of fittings	2	days
post-construction services	2	months

www.1adruck.at

Printing presses

3,20 m

19,23 sqm

1,60 m

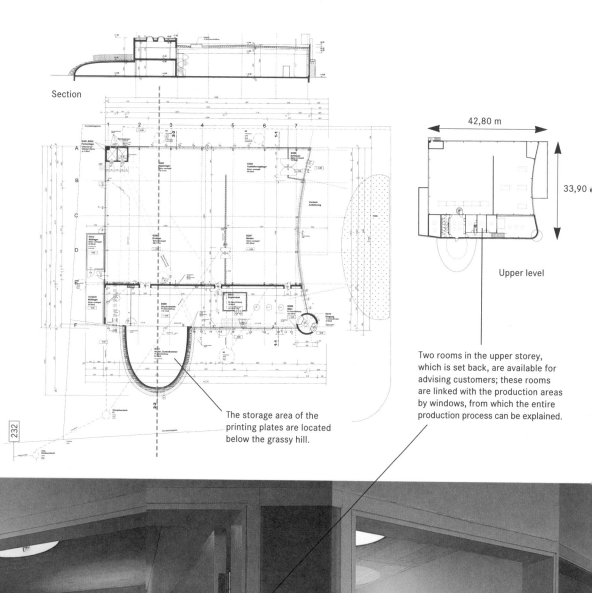

Section

42,80 m

33,90

Upper level

The storage area of the printing plates are located below the grassy hill.

Two rooms in the upper storey, which is set back, are available for advising customers; these rooms are linked with the production areas by windows, from which the entire production process can be explained.

21,10 sqm

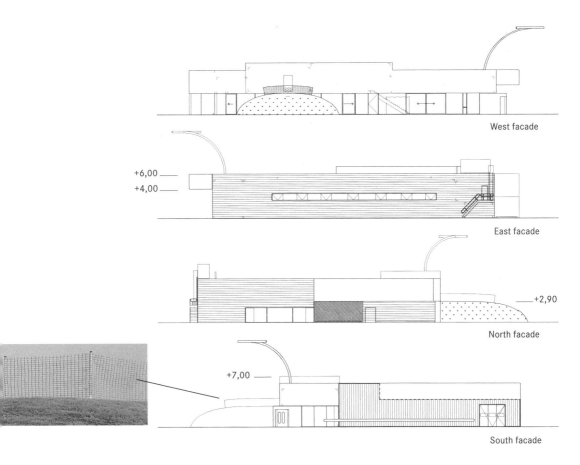

West facade

+6,00 ——
+4,00 ——

East facade

+2,90

North facade

+7,00 ——

South facade

Architects: "Too much trash, too few details"
LOVE: "Details were not part of the briefing"
It is one of the cheapest buildings of its kind in Steiermark.

The end

Entrance of the offices

> VERB

In all senses, the southern vertex of the Ljubljana-Graz-Zagreb triangle is formed by this last city. Zagreb is where Helena and Hrvoje Njiric work. njiric+njiric also seek a fluid relationship between architecture and consumer cultures in the information age. However, their desire to innovate comes up against incomprehension and immobility, and they are obliged to export their work to Slovenia in the face of the impossibility of building in their own country. Numerous second prizes and commissions frustrated at the last moment are confirmation of this. The Slovenian city of Maribor is at the midpoint of the triangle, very near the Croatian border. It is here that njiric+njiric have finally been able to materialize a MacDonald's restaurant (see LjubljanaLeibnitzMaribor) and their project for commercial premises for the Austrian do-it-yourself and construction company Baumaxx.

From the moment njiric + njiric won the competition convoked by Maribor Town Council for the construction of this hypermarket on a plot of land strategically situated on one of the main access routes into the town, Hrvoje and Helena Njiric entered into a long and tiring process of negotiation with the work's developer and client, a process which ended, more or less happily, in the sampling of the cake at the building's inauguration. This is the story we present below.

BAUMAXX HYPERMARKET. Tabor, Maribor
Built area: 12.500 sqm. (First phase built).
Client: Baumaxx Slovenia. Architects: njiric+njiric arhitekti. Hrvoje Njiric, Helena Njiric, Alan Kostrencic, Goran Tomas, Miljenco Stanic, Sinisa Glusica, Ivana Knez, Koraljka Brebric, Natasa Franciulla. Consultor: Bogdan Budimirov. Structure: Büro DI Franz Karisch (Völkermarkt, Austria). General Contractor: Stuag AG (Austria). Photographs: Damir Fabijanic, architects' archive.

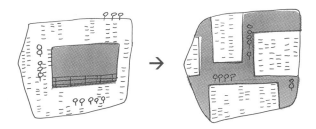

Maribor, 1997: An urban concept of reversing the figure/ground ratio of American hypermarkets. A celebration of traffic, performed by cutting the regular parking patterns into the irregular plot contour, should be strengthened by the green roof substance, as a new elevated ground, publicly accessible.

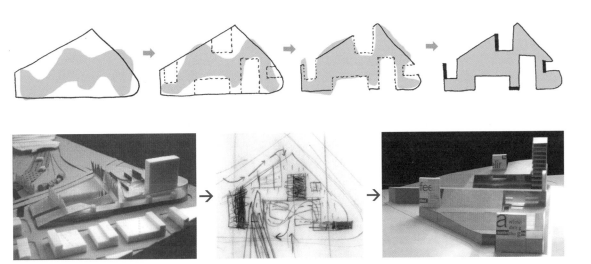

Maribor, 1999: The negative reaction of the developer turned the former concept into the new perceptual reality – no trespassing. The landscape is thus to be observed/mentally consumed/remote-controlled. The surreal nature of fireplace on the roof terrace of Beistegui apartment by Le Corbusier is equaled by the virtual status of the landscaped zone in the Hypermarket.

njiric+njiric > Here are a few summarizing excerpts from a huge correspondence we have had with the Austrian client (Baumaxx – Schoemerhaus) and the Austrian contractor (STUAG) for the Baumaxx Hypermarket in Maribor. It bears witness to an exemplary procedure – a series of negotiations, starting with the urban concept and leading to every single detail. It is a process that lasted from January 1997 to the fall of 1999 and was an enormous effort for the office in terms of costs and human resources.

Nevertheless, the game of compromising on every reasonable point and insisting on the very essential ones has resulted in a building which reflects all these iterations. We think that this set of alternative solutions has led to a new quality. It is the fate of architects: having to deal with hard-core consumerism of low-budget supermarket chains all over Europe – a feature that will come to account for an ever greater percentage of architectural production, given the lack of more attractive investors. Furthermore, the transitional countries of Eastern and Central Europe are facing the threat of a new-age colonialism. We have to learn its mechanisms to be able to interpret it in an acceptable manner.

01.97 > First contact with Stuag – proposal for shopping centre made.

02.97 > Baumaxx is the only known end user. Their brief consists of a one-storey building surrounded by a ground-level car park. Considering the importance of this 13,000 sqm site as regards its location in the city, we insist on the building having more than one level, with a tower acting as a landmark for this point of entry into the city and a roof-top car park reached by a ramp on the north side. The roof has to be a green zone to comply with the landscaping conditions set forth in the competition proposal.

03.97 > A second design has been drawn up that satisfies the requirements of Baumaxx and isn't too far removed from the winning proposal: the car park has been located on the roof and a single row of parking is allowed on the Tito Street side; the tower as a landmark for this approach to the city has been maintained; the roof is green in accordance with the landscaping requirements of the competition.

04.97 > Baumaxx don't want to locate the car park on the roof because of the existence of skylights there and for reasons of security against burglary. They are also unkeen on visitors to other neighbouring facilities parking there and thus gaining access to their roof.

05.97 > The architects draw up a third proposal in which the parking area is located in front of the building on several levels; the roof is kept as a green area; the active frontage is defined with triangular-section prismavision sheets – the building is really just an advertising megascreen. Baumaxx don't accept this variant of the project. The car park has to be located only and at street level, and the frontage can't be built with prismavision sheets because of their high cost.

07.97 > Meeting with Baumaxx in Celje (Slovenia). New brief – the built surface is to be extended.

08.97 > Meeting with Baumaxx in Klosterneuburg. A fourth proposal is presented in accordance with the programme established in July. Baumaxx agrees to an underground car park; the roof is kept green as stipulated in the competition; the tower is also retained as a landmark for the approach to the city.

information on
previous page

09.97 > Meeting with Baumaxx in Klosterneuburg and Zagreb. All the elements that define the shape of the project have been agreed on and presented to the Planning Committee as part of the site documentation. There are to be four illuminated billboards which will be very important for the formal definition of such a large building; the roof is green and landscaped; the tower marking the entrance to the city is retained as an office building.

10.97 > Baumaxx present the detailed brief for the fitting and finishing of the buildings – it becomes clear that it will be difficult to make the project coincide with the demands of the promoters. Baumaxx want a "yellow band" at a height of 1.2 m right round all the frontages of their building. We inform Stuag that to date we have made 13 variants of the project in order to meet the demands of Baumaxx. We put forward a new proposal for the frontage: the whole building will have a yellow façade – a polycarbonate outer coating will cover a layer of yellow mineral wool insulation.

11.97 > Stuag provide the architects with the composition and the layers of the green roof. This information has been incorporated into the final design.

02.98 > The application for planning permission is submitted.

03.98 > The treatment of the frontage as detailed in the final design technically meets all current legislation, and all the necessary permission is granted. The members of the competition panel have given written approval for the incorporation of all the changes made. Meeting with Baumaxx in Klosterneuburg. The billboards pose a problem in that Baumaxx use standard ones. Moreover, we think Baumaxx won't allow advertising by other companies on their roof.

04.98 > The City Council agrees to the granting of building permits in phases, as the promoters have asked to pay only for phase 1, corresponding to Baumaxx, and Baumaxx don't want to share the site with other facilities. We fear that only the part of the project that corresponds to Baumaxx will be built, which would be disastrous for such an important location. We ask the municipal authorities to get a commitment from Stuag that the project will be completed in its entirety.

20.04.98 > We ask Stuag for written conformity with the execution of the project by phases. We receive a fax from Stuag stating that the building will be completed in its totality only when buyers or leaseholders can be found.

08.05.98 > Meeting in Klosterneuburg with Baumaxx. Presentation of the CAD perspectives of the frontages for Baumaxx. Guarantees and details of the frontage are requested.

27.05.98 > The firm Almont of Slovenska Bistrica confirm the details and submit the detailed technical description of the proposed solution.

08.06.98 > Stuag tell us that Baumaxx don't accept the proposed frontage and ask for one of the following three proposals: façade coated with trapezoidal plate, brickwork façade with a monolayer finish, or façade of prefabricated concrete panels. Stuag decides that the frontage will be in prefabricated concrete panels, as this is the cheapest alternative.

The final finish of the facade on page 244.
www.rna.hr/98/HN-bau-HI2.htm

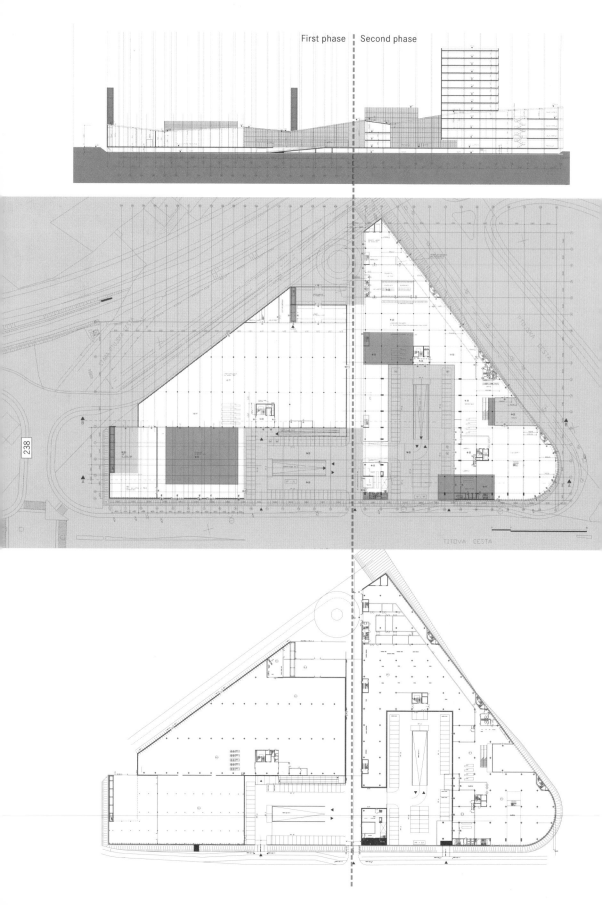

First phase | Second phase

10.06.98 > We warn Stuag about the possible consequences of changing documentation once it has been approved, as regards both the walls and the structure.

12.06.98 > Stuag reply that the changes will be solved "as we come to them".

22.06.98 > Misunderstanding about the green roof: the roof has to be actually planted out, not just given a green-coloured finish. The selection of frontages has been reduced to concrete prefabricated panels or a combination of these and trapezoidal plate.

02.07.98 > Talks with the prefabricated concrete panel manufacturer in Maribor.

09.07.98 > Following our meeting of 02.07 we fax Stuag to inform them that their demands have made it impossible to reach any formal definition of the prefabricated concrete panels, and have effectively limited the outer treatment of the elements of the frontage to the application of one coat of paint (!!!). According to the solution requested by the promoters, all the prefabricated concrete panels will have thermal bridges at all their joints, which goes against all the norms of the trade and clearly ignores current Slovenian legislation. We have told the promoters that we are unable to accept the responsibility for this type of error.

17.07.98 > Stuag inform us, without taking into account the logic of the structure, that the skylights have to be turned 90°, and that the roof will only have a green-coloured surface finish.

07.08.98 > Permission is granted to start the building work. The documentation that will be followed for the construction of the building differs from the documents originally presented in four main points:

1. Structure: the structural span has been extended from 6 to 12 metres and the secondary load-bearing elements, initially to be steel overlapped joints, have been replaced by prefabricated concrete beams.
2. External walls: the prefabricated concrete elements are suspended from the columns instead of resting on the floor. Their composition has been reduced to sandwich boards with a central layer of expanded polystyrene (6+8+6 cm), which doesn't meet Slovenian standards.
3. The surface area of the openings for natural ventilation has been reduced by 50% in the roof and 70% in the walls.
4. The structural design hasn't taken into account the load of the green roof.

28.08.98 > Fax from MR Projekt (Maribor) to tell us that the prefabricated concrete panels don't comply with current legislation.

07.09.98 > We submit new plans to Stuag incorporating the changes requested, although they will not be valid to start the building work until they comply to current Slovenian legislation.

11.09.98 > The promoters announce that they are scrapping the project for the office block.

22.09.98 > We send Stuag the colour scheme for the frontages, in accordance with requirements of Baumaxx.

13.10.98 > The Regional Planning Institute faxes all the parties involved to tell us what changes to the final design are unacceptable.

03.11.98 > Meeting with Stuag in Klagenfurt. Agreement reached on the <u>prefabricated concrete panels, the landscaped roof</u> (which will be in artificial turf and not planted out) and the construction of the billboards, which will be in either internally lit Plexiglas or externally lit wire fabric. The colour scheme is subject to confirmation by Baumaxx.

09.11.98 > Meeting with Baumaxx in Klosterneuburg. A new colour scheme is signed. The architects accept it on condition that all the billboards go ahead as planned.

17.11.98 > Meeting at the Regional Planning Institute. The authorities agree to Stuag and Baumaxx not erecting one of the billboards in this phase. Given the role played by the billboards in the overall design, the architects think that the competition committee should judge to what extent so many things can be eradicated from the initial design on the grounds of cost-cutting by the promoters, who were well acquainted with the project from the start. With this in mind, below we provide a list of the savings that, according to prices quoted by Stuag, all these changes have meant for the promoters.

PRICES AND SAVINGS (in Euros)

1. SAVINGS		
Polycarbonate frontage + insulation 3,300 sqm 3,300 x € 113.04 = € 373.04	Prefabricated concrete 3,300 x € 78.49 = € 259,005.98	Difference +€ 114,034.58
Landscaped roof 5,630 sqm 5,630 x € 36.34 + € 50,879.98 = € 221,288.78	Artificial turf 5,630 x € 14.53 = € 81,829.61	Difference +€ 139,459.17
Steel structure 23 frames x 12/18 m: 23 x € 12.07 = € 277,638.71	Concrete 23 x € 7,912.62 = € 181,990.22	Difference +€ 95,648.50
2. COSTS		
Billboard II 540 sqm: 540/1,245 x € 581,382.67 = –€ 252,320.08		
Coloured concrete + finish of frontages 2,000 sqm: 2,000 x € 14.53 = –€ 29,069.13		
3. TOTAL (SAVINGS – COSTS)		
€ 114,034.58 + € 139,459.17 + € 95,648.50 = € 252,320.08 + € 29,069.13 =		+€ 349,142.24 –€ 281,418.28
DIFFERENCE =		+€ 67,753.03

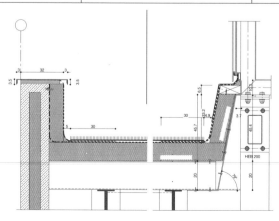

Maribor > City Council. Regional Planning Institute. Minutes of the meeting held on 12.01.99

The following agreements are reached:
1. Support is given to the protection of the integrity of the competition proposal, and also to the solution in its totality.
2. The changes made in the documentation of the final design are unjustified, especially those made to the façade.
3. The construction of the transformer station is considered to be a detail that should be agreed between the architects and the promoters.
4. In phase 2 of the construction of the complex the roof should be made transitable, and it is lamented that this idea has not been pursued in phase 1.
5. The final layer of the roof built in phase 1 should be artificial turf.
6. The promoters should finalize the budgetary arrangements with the architects, and they should respect both the importance of the site for the city and the following requirements:
- The billboards must be maintained, as must the number of them, although they may be constructed differently.
- The frontage should be transparent, being constructed in glass, plastic, etc.
- Any changes in the project must first obtain the appropriate permits.

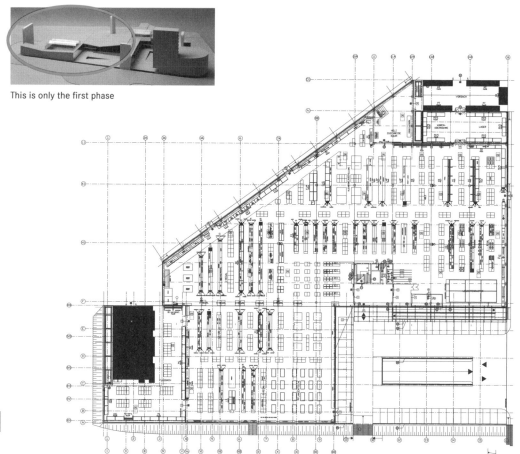

This is only the first phase

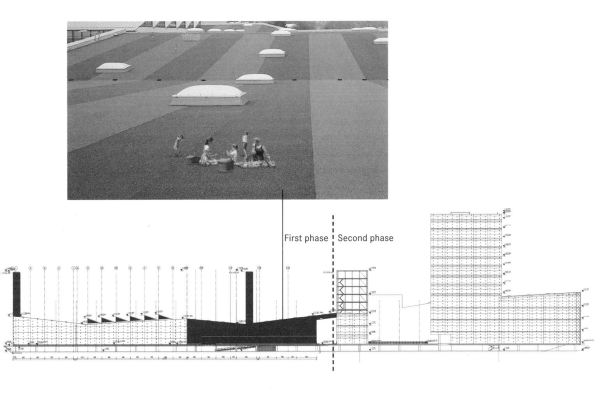

First phase | Second phase

All inward-bound planes are entirely glazed, and all perimeter ones are mute. A green roof as a common denominator and recreated artificial topography. Four billboards "anchor" the vast slopes of the House to the site and turn to the traffic streams.

We think of a house in its natural appearance: wood is wood, brick is brick, concrete is concrete. Even the glazed elevations from the first facade concept (October 97) exploited the properties of insulating wool as such. We used its yellowness as a part of the Baumaxx corporate identity, simply attaching the red logos to it and blurring them slightly with corrugated polycarbonate sheets.

Color as a marketing strategy.
In the theory of visual communications yellow and red are considered as "cheap", low-budget colors.
That is why such D-I-Y markets use them.

It was decided to remain in the realm of readymades by choosing to put a layer of custom-made traffic reflectors in signal red and silver atop of concrete. The op-art effect is addressed to the drivers as a major circulation force on the spot. Such a kinetic experience of the envelope — silver from the north, red from the south, neutral from the west, blends with the firm's corporate colors. In the night the House turns to the pure Light.

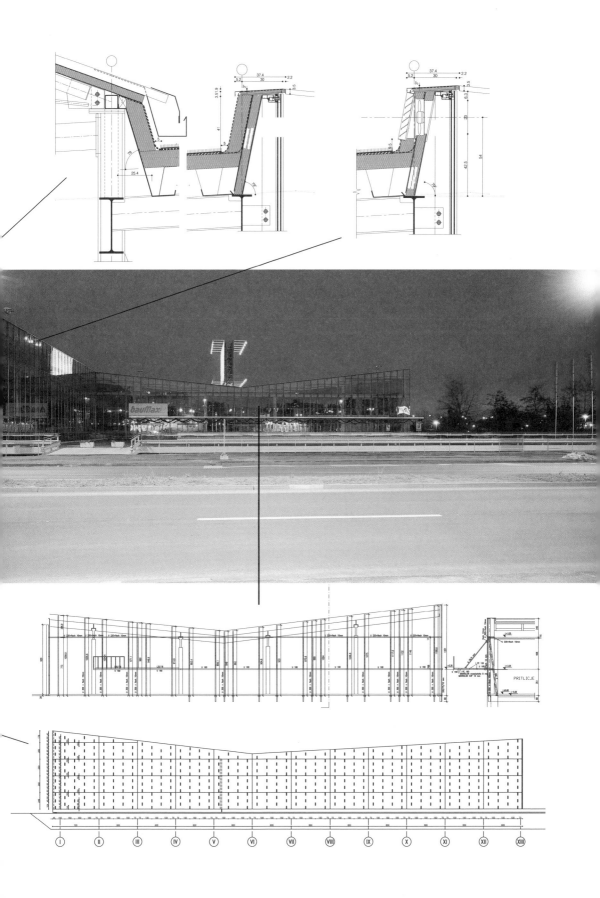

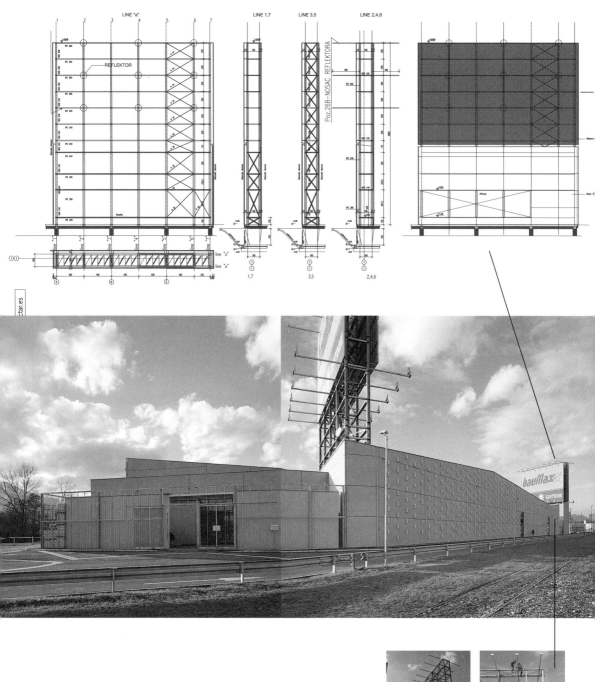

And here, gentlemen, behind this placard,
is the university town of Maribor…

Immediately after completion, the Slovenes "discovered" unparalleled similarity with the oeuvre of The Father. What came out of necessity to resolve the tensions of the site and objectives of the program, was suddenly seen as a blasphemous remake of Plečnik (the Church of the Holy Heart – Prague 1933). Should a comparable design – in overall layout and formulation of the skin, really be prosecuted? Although we had never considered it as referential to our project, the hints put forward by the high priests of the Plečnik religion made us think. Isn't a temple of Christianity the right typological ancestor for the house of contemporary religion – that of consumer? What are parallels like – entrance Baumaxx panel / statue of St Mary over main doors, or bell-tower/billboard – but a document of shifted social concerns from the spiritual to the material? Could the Venturi-like semiotics testify to the similar system of signifiers, appropriated for the masses?

And finally, isn't it easier for the non-Slovenes to terminate the Oedipal relation and "liberate" them from the heavy load of the father-figure? Furthermore, opening a public debate on the validity of architectural concepts in current production indicates the high level of concern of the Slovene culture scene, as well as the capacity of the very building to provoke such intensities.

Is there any possible link between <u>bricolage and architecture</u>? Bricolage is a particular form of communication between objects and authors. According to Sherry Turkle it means a flexible, negotiated, non-hierarchical way of working. Computer interfaces, for example, follow the bricoleur logic: a limited number of objects and tools enable the user to perform an unlimited number of results.

Sherry Turkle is Professor of Sociology at the Massachusetts Institute of Technology. She is the author of *Life on the Screen: Identity in the Age of the Internet* (New York: Simon and Schuster, 1995. Paperback edition, New York: Touchstone, 1997), and has written numerous articles on psychoanalysis and culture and on the "subjective side" of people's relationships with technology, especially computers. See http://web.mit.edu/sturkle/www

The end

00251

A

Romance au bord du Lac

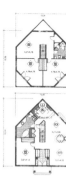

03775

B

Polygonale

08125

AA

01428

E

250

> VERB

The house is a problematic instance of the relationship between the output of architects and the inhabitants of this. Bricolage, on the other hand, is a structure of communication that works. It works better than most relationships between clients and architects. Is a bricolage-architecture possible that can bring the inhabitant closer to the resulting architecture? Or the architect to the other elements implicated in the design, materialization or use of houses?

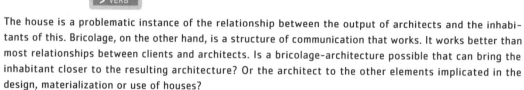

Contemporaine

Belle de Ville

BB

06113

Philosophe

A

07501/ 07504

La Diplomate

Source: *Planimage, en Maison. Décors & Intérieurs*, April-May-June 2000, no.6, Paris.

Grenoble

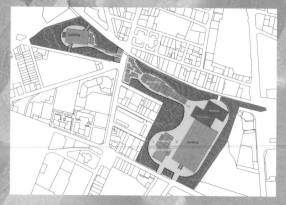

← G. Pompidou Park

Rue de Stalingrad

Grenoble has faced the repercussions of the late 20th century modernization to which the surrounding countryside has submitted itself. The self-strengthening mechanism of concentration has changed in dynamic decentralization: the town has spread throughout the region, but has been stopped by the surrounding mountains.

Since housing has moved from inner cities, the erosion has advanced at a more rapid pace. After the medium-sized business came the shopping centers, then the service industries, the industrial estates and business parks, research laboratories, the technology centers, the recreational institutions and the leisure and sport establishments. All these facilities are now situated in the area between the old center and the mountain slopes.

The ideal of the inhabitants of Grenoble is to live on the green slopes of the mountains. Living in the green surroundings stands for freedom, individuality and status.

It seems as if there is a conflict between the city and its green surroundings. The city-dweller has a primary interest in the political, economic and social life found in the public life of the city. The autonomy of nature is sacrificed for cultural dynamics and progress.

At the same time, people need a private world, away from social demands. Withdrawn from the city, their own individual houses foster their green space and the countryside, which represents everything that is 'unspoiled' and salubrious.

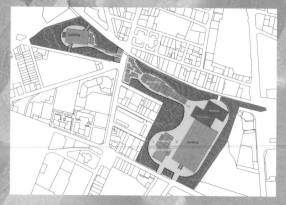
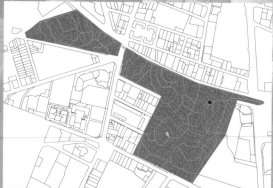

HILLCITY: Proposal for the competition "Dwelling in the year 2000", September 2000
Koerszeinstravangelderen architecten: Ira Koers, Jurjen Zeinstra, Mikel van Gelderen, Katrin Blass, Charlotte Kokken, Menno Veldman

Artificial hills

Individual gardens

Individual self-build houses

Rue des Alliés

Small, winding footpaths

Rue de Stalingrad cuts through the hill, so that the leisure and shopping facilities can be easily reached by the pedestrian in the existing street.

The hills are filled for the greater part with a commercial urban program. Most of this interior world is hidden, but at some crucial places the hills open up and show their real inside to the city.

All the houses on the hills are linked to an internal system of stairs and elevators that connects the car park to the houses.

The proposal creates a new landscape that stretches between the existing green areas. In its most literal form the two worlds are piled up; the dynamic, commercial world of infrastructure, shopping and leisure is completely covered by the quiet green world of individual hillside housing.

View of the surrounding mountains

'Ordinary and banal' housing

After the experience of the 'grand ensembles' at the sixties, the governments no longer create large-scale housing projects. Housing is nowadays carefully located within the existing urban structure and helps to improve its quality. The once active role of the government has been taken over by the market within close cooperation with central and local authorities.

Outside downtown, there has always been a strong demand for individual houses, with a garden and a parking space, preferably situated on the green hillside. Planners and architects have long resented this form of 'ordinary and banal' housing, but today there is a growing conviction that there can be some unexplored qualities in this form of spontaneous housing and their aesthetics of deregulation. Especially within the urban context this seemingly anti-urban form of housing might offer a new challenge for the city, when it is subjected to certain conditions.

Seville

> VERB

Real. Ingenious. Direct. Unaesthetic. Everyday. Cheap. This alternative occupation in an apartment block is a bricolage as real as TV soaps in the afternoon. And on top of that it's absolutely legal. Methodically and as far as is possible, it utilizes the law and the regulations to arrive at a totally different configuration of an apartment, one that's parasitical on its neighbors. In this instance, with all planning permissions in order.

LEGAL BASIS

1. Partial rental contract for an apartment.

This type of contracts are regulated by Law 29/1994, November 24, Urban Rentals. As this deals with housing rentals, in the absence of the cited law, the wishes of the parties involved will be enforced, supplemented by the provisions of the Civil Code (art. 4 LAU).

The contracts which can be entered into are of two types. One, a rental contract for a part of a property owned by the lessor, and the other a rental contract for a sublet of part of a property, in which we are subject to certain conditions previously set between the lessor and the lessee who later subleases (art. 8 LAU).

2. Installation of circulation conduits in light wells.

In the case which concerns us here, an interpretation of articles 7 and 12 of the horizontal property law, in terms permitted by art. 3.1 of the Civil Code, leads us to affirm that the use of the facades of the interior light wells to locate the circulation conduits, not placed in a permanent or fixed manner, but rather moveable, permitting their easy disassembly and removal, cannot be considered inappropriate by the co-owner of the said lightwell, but rather as a rational and justified use of the cited communal element, which in no way implies the alteration of the same. (see, Sentence of 8-6-1998, no. 171/1998, Provincial Court of Murcia, Section 1ª).

By its nature and characteristics this installation doesn't ostensibly effect the configuration or appearance of the building, nor its construction or security, and neither does it cause damages to the other owners of the building, nor does it impede their use of other common elements, as is reflected in the construction project.

According to article 394 C.C., each participant is allowed to use the common spaces, always when they are used for their intended purpose and in such a way as not to damage the interests of the community, and not impede that the other owners use them as is their right. Not being established in the statutes of the community or in the rules of the interior management any specific use for the repeated interior lightwell, there exists no problem in locating the elements described in the project, with the necessary authorization of the board of owners, in light of the above and by requirement of art. 17 of the horizontal property law it will require the approval by one third of the members of the community, representing one third of the property.

In the event that the elements are installed without attaining the indicated majority approval or not soliciting this approval, there exists sufficient basis to file a claim against the community, protected by the above stated arguments and the existence of antecedents in the community, when chimneys for smoke ventilation from businesses in the ground floor were installed without the authorization of the board, and which are centers of noise, smoke and heat and which clearly are more bothersome for the property owners.

3. Installation of architectural furniture on the roof.

The placement of this element on the building roof, as it affects a common space — which cannot be sub-divided (art. 396 C.C) — renders this a private use which affects the other community members and therefore requires the unanimous consent of the owner's board (it is constantly demonstrated that this quorum is attained on very few occasions, even in the case of modifications which would be advantageous to all property owners).

Deciding to install the module without the consent of the owner's board, the president of the community should require us to remove it, with the warning that in the case of non-compliance appropriate measures would be taken. To file a preliminary claim before the local court it will be necessary to attach an affidavit of the summons and a certification of the motion adopted by the owner's board which must be a majority of the community of owners. All this must take place in a period of between 4 and 6 months.

In the event that the judgment of the petition is completely in favor of the community, ruling against the right to install the kit, we would have to return the roof to its former state and, if it was the case, pay damages. In our case in particular, or that of the neighbors who support our proposal to occupy the roof, no damages will be required due to the design of the module to be installed.

Signed. IGNACIO PRETEL. Lawyer.

HABITABLE STRUCTURE. 11, Residencial Conde Bustillo
Maximum cost: € 2.910. Client developer: Santiago Cirugeda. Graphic design: Valle Piñero, Javier Roman. Architect: Santiago Balbontín.
Legal consultant: Ignacio Pretel. Building company: Recicapa

CLIENT DEVELOPER

The following project was prepared, as commissioned by me, Santiago Cirugeda Parejo, resident of apartment 6B and with the power of attorney vested in me by the owner of the apartment, D. Miguel Cirugeda Marcet.

The objective of this project is to find a legal and constructional structure to permit the connection of spaces belonging to different property owners of the same apartment building, constituted and regulated by the Law of Horizontal Property and the Civil Code. This involves an investigation of the possibilities of development and derivation which can be produced under the jurisdiction of this law. The final object being the construction of a habitable spatial configuration running invisibly through the affected building.

A series of spatial configurations are generated, as defined by means of partial rental contracts with the owners of the neighboring apartments, who cede for my use rooms or fragments of rooms (sqm), and by the installation of circulation conduits in the building's interior light wells (specified as common spaces by the Law of Horizontal Property).

The present project describes the work, both of mechanical systems and renovations, agreed upon with the following property owners, 4A, 5B, 6A and 7B. The decision of construction dates for particular parts of the project affecting their property, depended on each owner's process and vital necessities, converting the structure in something changing and progressive; developing how and when it would, linking its size and evolution to the personal and legal relationships which the below signed maintains with the different neighbors.

The variable occupation of the roof using architectural furniture kits by Architectural Games S.C. 670794409 is dependent on the difficult unanimous consensus of the owners community, and in its absence a judicial process which could be attempted by different petitioners.

Signed. SANTIAGO CIRUGEDA. CLIENT

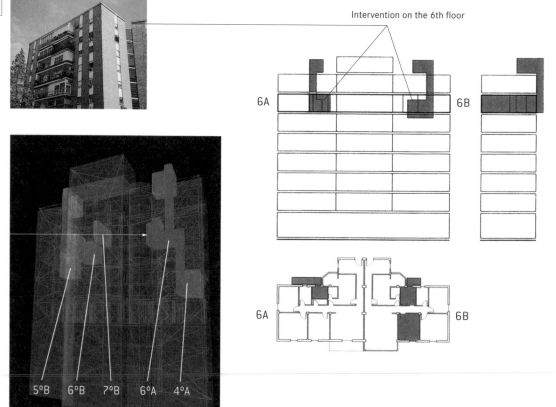

Intervention on the 6th floor

6A   6B

6A   6B

5ºB   6ºB   7ºB   6ºA   4ºA

ARCHITECTURAL CONDITIONS

Location
Apartments 6B, 4A, 5B, 6A, 7B, which are affected by the current project are located in building 11 of the Residencia Conde de Bustillo, whose overall structure consists of two other buildings which are interconnected by common garden and parking areas.

Background information
The building in which the renovations and installation of exterior circulation conduits will be made has a concrete structure of poured in place columns and floor slabs of pre-cast joists and pre fabricated ceramic floor units. It is made up of a ground floor with commercial spaces plus 7 floors of apartments and an accessible roof, organized in three parts which share a common circulation and mechanical core, as well as 3 interior light wells.

Improvements and electrical systems
The renovations and mechanical systems to be installed in each property are specified in the unit take off and budget of each particular case, and are divided into the following sections:
Demolition: slabs, walls and interior partitions.
Interior construction: construction of double-sided partitions using studs and wallboard, insulation boards and fill.
Painting: Painted finishes with texture and color to be determined by each individual.
Circulation conduit: Conduit made of 40 x 40 x 4 mm galvanized metal sections clad with insulated forexpan panels, including aluminum ladder and chemical anchors.
Electricity: The electrical system, consisting of the electrical outlets and illumination of the different spatial units, will use butyl protected cable and 2,5 sqmm (nom.) minimum section conduit, using the electrical panel in apartment 6B.
Kit: eventually an architectural furniture kit by Arch.Games.S.C. will be installed on the roof, with no anchors or fasteners being attached to the same.
Structural modifications will not be made in any of the partial projects, excepting the openings in floor slabs for the interior conduits, which will be opened between joists with dimensions 65 x 100 cm.

Signed. SANTI BALBONTIN. ARCHITECT.

Kit includes:
- two 2000 x 1000 mm platforms of 60 x 60 x 4 mm galvanized steel sections
- four 4000 mm vertical supports of 60 x 60 x 4 mm galvanized steel sections
- ten 80x5 mm curved galvanized steel plate ribs
- twelve 2000 x 1000 x 5 mm sheets of white PVC (forex)
- two 2000 x 1000 x 21 mm sheets of plywood
- Fasteners and assembly diagram.
- Architectural furniture which can be disassembled and reused with different conceptual and constructional options. Demonstrating the fuzzy distinction between ephemeral architecture and furniture construction.

- Different real options for use are shown, where the construction frame and the different conditions for purpose and function demonstrate a varied series of options:
- Temporary home extensions. (scaffolding)
- Compact exhibit gallery for non-professionals. (capsule)
- Element of modulation and image for a young peoples clothing store. (underwear storage).

COST ESTIMATE: QUOTATION OF THE INTERVENTION IN APARTMENT 4A.

SECTIONS: DEMOLITION. INTERIOR CONSTRUCTION. PAINTING. CONDUITS. ELECTRICITY AND KIT.
Manual demolition of a 25 cm. thick double wall consisting of one wythe of brick+air space+partition, including removal and transportation of remaining material and patching with M-4 cement mortar. Existing area measured.
€ 11,6/sqm x 1,3 sqm   € 15,08

Y-25 wallboard partition 13 x 2 mm thick over 46 mm cellular cardboard core, with finish dimension 98 mm covering the entire floor to ceiling height and attached to a substructure of galvanized steel, including layout, sub-framing, screws, cleaning, leveling, finishing of corners and joints, constructed per NTE/PTP and specifications of the panel manufacturer. Measured lineally.
€ 31,91/sqm x 1,56 sqm   € 49,78

Skim coat of plaster on walls, with trowel applied pearlescent plaster, built according to NTE/RPQ-12, Measured lineally, without reductions.
€ 8,48/sqm x 3,9 sqm   € 33,07

Smooth latex paint on horizontal surfaces and brick, plaster and concrete vertical surfaces. Including sanding and cleaning of substrate, primer coat, patching, a second primer coat and two finish coats according to NTE/RPP-24. Executed area measured.
€ 5,02/sqm x 3,9 sqm   € 19,59

Partition for personal circulation conduit, constructed of 26 mm (3+20+3) panels of forexpan structured by LC 40 x 40 x 4 mm cold galvanized steel sections, including installation, auxiliary aluminum ladder and chemical anchors. Executed area measured.
€ 32,63/sqm x 16,6 sqm (connection with 6A)   € 541,74.
€ 32,63/sqm x 27,3 sqm (direct connection)   € 890,93

Electrical circuit for illumination and other uses, using three 2,5 sqmm (nom.) minimum section wires in a butyl protected cable, surface mounted, including required junction boxes and galvanized steel fasteners. Executed length measured from the electrical panel or the corresponding junction box to the junction box in the last room fed.
€ 2,06/ml x 39 ml   € 80,63

Unit surface mounted 10/16 A circuit with ground, installed using butyl protected cable with three 2,5 sqmm (nom.) minimum section conduits, surface mounted, including first quality accessories, required junction boxes, anchors and fasteners, built according to NTE/IEB-50. Finished unit measured.
€ 10,51/ud x 3 ud   € 31,55

SUMTOTAL SECTIONS (connection 6A)   € 771,45
SUMTOTAL SECTIONS (direct connection)   € 1120,65

OPCIONAL (legal conditions)
Unit KIT n°1 of the "architectural furniture" series by ARCHITECTURAL GAMES S.C. 670794409:
Mobile and demountable 4 x 2,3 x 2,5 m module consisting of a metal structure clad in forexpan   € 601,01

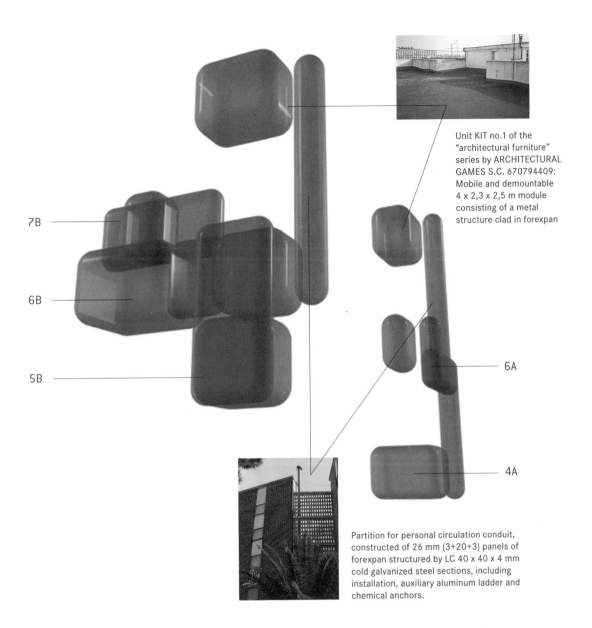

7B

6B

5B

6A

4A

Unit KIT no.1 of the "architectural furniture" series by ARCHITECTURAL GAMES S.C. 670794409: Mobile and demountable 4 x 2,3 x 2,5 m module consisting of a metal structure clad in forexpan

Partition for personal circulation conduit, constructed of 26 mm (3+20+3) panels of forexpan structured by LC 40 x 40 x 4 mm cold galvanized steel sections, including installation, auxiliary aluminum ladder and chemical anchors.

And from reality to total fiction. Anton Markus Pasing was already talking about this on page 122 during the TV ads. Now he describes an invasion. Parasite robots take over the residential areas around our cities. It can happen at any moment...

262

Happy neighbors

We love it!

Garden gnome

For information on the garden gnome liberation front, see www.internettrash.com/users/sprkythdvl/gnome.htm

Parasites   Anton Markus Pasing

Again we had a full moon, the night was peaceful, and a light mist hovered above the suburb. But the silence was deceptive, the scene was invaded from far away by a muffled metallic pounding. The idyll threatened to be overturned.

Agile and selfish 'machines-for-living-in' took the suburbs of large cities by surprise in their search for a new home – the front garden.

Once they had arrived there, they operated their sensor-controlled boring heads to dock onto the supply lines laid between the street and the suburban villa. They went to anchor in the grounds and thus threatened to poison the ground water and to soil the automobile, should residents try to take action against them.

There was a colossal uproar amongst decent upper-middle-class citizens in subsequent weeks, but when they realized that 'nothing and nobody' could do anything against these housing robots and that they were even quite useful, the clamor subsided.

The parasites monitored the grounds in high-tech fashion and successfully thwarted any attempts to break in and rob their hosts:

They sprayed potential criminals with a foul-smelling sticky synthetic substance or else paralyzed them by means of a kind of sonic boom canon until the official guardians of law and order had rushed to the scene.

And when the parasites finally started spouting cute little garden gnomes (nobody knew, though, that these were made of tightly compressed parasitic waste matter) the tables turned and everybody suddenly craved for a parasite! A new status symbol had seen the light of day, and the symbiosis was complete.

Life returned to normal, even though the municipal building supervisors untiringly thundered against these 'itinerant scrap heaps' – but who cared! (And what did these people know about architectural culture anyway?!)

In short, a new harmony established itself: peace on earth.

And so the parasites lived happily ever after!

————————————— criminal repellent by spraying a foul-smelling sticky synthetic substance

————————————— waste matter compressor and garden gnomes spouter device

————————————— sonic boom canon

————————————— sensor-controlled boring head

Verb to Do

This issue is all about processes and interactions which redefine the notion of authorship. For many people this is no news. Many people are talking about this these days and have talked about this before – even of course back in the 1960s. >>> But most of this talk takes place only among artists and designers. Architects are lagging behind. One of the many inspiring sources of ideas for this issue is the activity being carried out by 'do' – a brand, a community, an idea. If you have not yet heard of 'do', please read on. >>> Although maybe you have seen or heard of the 'do create' exhibition, or of its A3 catalogue. This exhibition featured a series of house products which require user's participation for them to be of any use. These products were presented at the International Furniture Fair 2000 in Milan, and then in the 'do create' exhibition which has travelled – so far – to the Kunsthal in Rotterdam, Colette in Paris, the Rocket Gallery in Tokyo, the AA School of Architecture in London, Teo Jakob Tagliabue in Geneva and The Apartment in New York. Some of these products – do scratch, do swing, do hit, do cut, do reincarnate, do frame, do break and do shirt – are now being commercially produced and sold throughout the world, probably at a store near you. >>> 'do create' was a collaboration between do and Droog Design, the innovative organization which stimulates discussion on design and whose proposals reached a wide audience in the late 1990s through the books published by Utrecht's Centraal Museum and by 010, Rotterdam (see www.droogdesign.nl). In his introduction to the 'do create' catalogue, Renny Ramakers from Droog Design explains what this project is about.

Renny Ramakers > "This project by Droog Design and do take you up a completely different road. The title, 'do create', is appealing to both designer and custormer: the designer creates a product and the customer then interacts with it. The designer creates a half-finished product so to speak, for the custormer to complete and add his or her own personal touch. It's an open design; things are left to chance and are beyond the control of the designer. The customer does not have to design from scratch and there are no preprogrammed contributions either. On the contrary, you buy a product, a design that you like, which you can work out for yourself and add you own interpretation to. In a number of cases, you really have to finish the product yourself.

(...) Users are invited to interact and play. They can influence the design. Products can thus become part of their personalities. You don't buy form, style or function: you buy an experience. It is what you do to the object or what the object does to you or makes you do that counts. 'do create' is characterised by very different consumer relationships.

The increasingly familiar notion of 'onthaasting', which tells you to 'stop hurrying', applies to many of these products. When you buy a 'do create' product, you must set to work, you lose time. Products sell at an amazing speed these days and consumers are stimulated to keep buying new things. Processes are no longer noticed. There is hardly any contact with matter. There is no patience for 'slow' and 'intricate'. Things must be easy and complete, to be taken in at a glance. They are cast aside so quickly that there is no time for any bond. The 'do create' products are at their best when a customer adds a bit of his own self. Sometimes this is rather simple, sometimes it is a matter of blood, sweat and tears. That this will create a relationship with the products is to be expected. But it doesn't come easy: you'll have to put in some effort. Buy 'do create' and you know what you're letting yourself in for. To do or not to do, that's the question."

Verb > But what is 'do'?

Joanna van der Zanden > "You may not have heard of this new brand, but you will, for sure, be very familiar with one of life's very simple lessons, something our mothers would have drummed into us at an early age: you can only make things happen by doing.
do, as the name suggests, is an ever-changing brand that depends on what you do.
A brand that is open to ideas from anyone and anywhere.
do would like to offer an antidote to the one-way world we live in, and therefore started with a simple proposition: to change the conventions of brands. Most brands would start by creating products or services and out of that, much later, would come the brand mentality. do turned this on its head and started with a philosophy and a dream. As an ever-changing brand, do is, by definition, always unfinished. do products or services or events can only exist with the interaction of consumers, brands and others who want to do.
You could say that do is as much a call to action as it is a brand – it's about living and doing – but do also wants to leave positive social footprints. The personality of do is non-conformist, socially critical, self-analytical, and aware, but do isn't exclusive. Everyone can get involved in helping make do; an inclusive brand open to the many rather than being produced by a select few.
By introducing the 'do create' collection, do hopes not only to inspire consumers to participate, but also manufacturers and other brands. do wants to be a platform for realising, along with other brands and companies, products/services/events which make people think and act.
You can read, click or watch more about do at www.dosurf.com. do hopes you enjoy and are inspired by 'do create' and looks forward to hearing from you...soon."

'DO' HAVE A DREAM

What does this future brand believe? do is all about being active and involved in the way the world works. This means social responsibility, concern for the planet, ideas for change, and a willingness to take action. It also means that you want to have fun and are maybe a little tired of the way things are usually done. Why do we drive cars with only four doors, when it might be fun to drive with 20? Why can't we make recycling profitable? Why can't washing powders change the colors of our shirts each time we wash them so that we have instantly new wardrobes? The possibilities are endless. All we have to do is do something.

> VERB

The website also reveals that do is an initiative of the Amsterdam communication agency KesselsKramer (www.kesselskramer.com), and that besides collaborating with Droog Design in 'do create', do made an impact in the world of media with an interactive TV project launched in Rotterdam on 2 February 2000 (see www.do-tv.com) and has published a few books. They can be ordered at www.dosurf.com. At Actar we like books, so we did order them. And *Verb* provides the opportunity to share their contents. What follows is an extract of the 3rd edition of the book *do future*, copyright © 1998-1999-2000, do Publishing Co., Inc., KesselsKramer Unlimited, all rights unreserved.

DO 1:1

What could be more enduring, or so it seems, than the familiar process of idea to realisation to the 'experiencing' thereof? For example, advertisers first draw up a concept, which is then worked out in detail, and then offered to the mass media for 'consumption.' The consumer is then permitted to swallow the easily digestible chunks. That's what happens now and has done, it seems, for centuries.

In cyberspace, the network world of tomorrow, which is supposed to minimise the broadcasting of today, creative people no longer think up easily digestible concepts in advance. Or no longer, at least, for masses of people simultaneously. This is no longer necessary and no longer possible. Why not?

To start with, it will no longer be necessary to get a preconceived message to catch the eye of the public which will then, using an idea as a catalyst to accelerate it, 'pervade and persuade people's minds.' The fragmentation, dynamics and the unpredictability of 'the masses' makes trying to think up an idea which will appeal to all of them a waste of time. Proposals are fragmenting too and becoming 1:1.

On the Net, everything happens simultaneously: thinking and doing, getting ideas and realising them, trying and learning, seeing/understanding and acting, sending and receiving – if you want to know what goes on in this world, just read the book Disclosure by Michael Crichton. Inside the network, communal meeting places are created; sometimes spontaneously, sometimes they are pre-arranged. Usually, the only thing that has been already put in place is an ambience or a setting which the participants can use to play their games or act out their dialogues. Certain conditions have been created and the building blocks have been made available – for example, theme worlds sponsored by suppliers of products or services – but the real creative work, i.e. te experience is created on-(web)site. For instance, those who make games realise that they no longer have to lay down a storyline; instead, all they have to do is arrange a few settings and place in them a few characters whose games you can join in. Ideas are then created from the experiences you have in these encounters. Thus, encounters on the Net will develop in the same way as when an artist with a generous, free spirit sees an idea which he or she has started work on ripen more and more to (clear-cut) fruition. The ideas currently on offer on the Net are small and short-lived. Bigger, long-running, clear-cut concepts are already thin on the ground. For example, the challenge to Just Do It (Nike) is more a thin corporate umbrella under which Nike can go its own way in any direction it pleases rather than a concept which is used to give the company its direction. Concepts are becoming weaker and weaker and more thematic. Concepts are becoming straitjackets for both their creators and consumers.

(By the way, when we say 'the Net', we mean the Great Network of Emotions, where Virtual Reality will enable us to do a great deal more than we can currently do at the glorified storage depots for text we call the Internet.)

On the Net, the only thing that counts is the experience of the here and now. Actions produce insights and ideas immediately. Thinking no longer precedes doing. Ideas no longer precede their realisation. It is also true that ideas are no longer created by creative people; instead, ideas arise in the interplay in the games and the dialogues.

This is a different situation to that of our linear communication process. We still see action as the taking of action based on a certain formula, a certain vision, a certain ideology, such as the communist ideology, or the ideology of belier. In the past, these ideologies were the 'epic stories,' such as those of Lenin and Marx. They formulated certain ideas, and many people conformed to these ideas. People's actions were in line with that model. The followers were driven on by the tyranny of that model. They were not allowed to have any ideas themselves. They became conditioned, dehumanised. The only thing you cared about were the concepts and their realisations. This mechanism still exists in advertising, in a somewhat toned-down form. In current society too, we feel that an elite formulates the ideas and that thought precedes action. Action is taken according to a pre-considered model, whether it be made up of ideas from the state or from a religion or from brands. These ideas are broadcast via the mass media. Buy this brand (i.e. idea) and it will make you happy or enable you to attain this lifestyle.

In actual fact, this is not taking action, at least not according to the notion of action as experience in the here and now. The only experiences that people undergo are the acts of purchasing and consumption; the rest is in their imagination – an illusion.

Thus we have a second, more ethical reason why commerce can no longer and should no longer interfere in people's sets of beliefs.

If we go back to the Greek word for idea, we discover that the word is connected with 'seeing.' Thus, the word 'idea' represents (in)sight, i.e. seeing and doing simultaneously. The 'click' movement occurs whilst we are in the process of taking action. It is not a case of seeing, drawing a conclusion from this and then acting accordingly. Nor is it: observing, developing a certain conviction (an idea, a formula) as the result of this observation, and then acting on the basis of this formula. If we act in this way then we have freed ourselves from the act of observation, in which case we are acting mechanically.

If seeing and doing occur simultaneously, then we experience infinite freedom. If they don't, then this is not freedom, which is why the communists said that freedom doesn't exist. Freedom is when you live in a world of concepts, not in a world of actions. This is what we do in the world of advertising concepts too – we think them up for people. It becomes impossible to gain insights through action if someone is offering preconceived ideas.

It is no longer about the best idea for a campaign or about being funny. It is about your having presence in the relationships, in discourse on the Net. When people are discussing hhow difficult it is to get sauces to thicken, a manufacturer can use an idea which has arisen at that moment and say at exactly the right moment: But I can do that for you! Just-in-time communication. No more little lessons to be learnt by heart in bulk.

Getting a uniform response from everybody has long been a dream. More and more advertising is already becoming 'open-ended': everybody can take the advert and go his or her own way with it. In doing so we are getting ahead of developments a little. However, it is only in cyberspace where it is really happening. This is where the technological pre-conditions (i.e. pressures) are arising for the democratisation of communication. Everybody creates their own world. Everybody is creative. There are no longer any creative specialists who are busy 'preconceiving ideas for you.' There are no longer any strategists either. Why should they in their turn be able to and have to steer the actions of the creative people? The 1:1 experience at the meeting places on the Net is the communal 'product.' The idea is an interaction – an action. Manufacturers can create the pre-conditions necessary for letting these experiences occur. However, we cannot then in all honesty call them 'products.' This is no longer what it is about, unlike in today's world, where many people still get worked up about what they see pouring off the end of the production line.

This is why you should look at a brand more as a mutual experience, as part of an interaction, than as something which the manufacturer controls (irrespective of whether this control is physical or emotional). In this way, every experience of insight and doing has become unique. In cyberspace, there will be as many brands as there are communal moments of experience. As a matter of fact, this means that brands will become processes; they will never end. They will never be completed. Everything is in the process of formation.

DO WRITE

If you are a publisher, out there in the world, publishing.
Contact do about doing a magazine.
A magazine about all the things people can do,
everyday

DO FUTURE IS:

do now to shape future.
There are two modes:
Do before you think.
Think before you do.
do future uses the second mode, unless you prefer chaos.
So *do future* is, Think Now.
Draw from all your experience
Or create new blocks
By doing before you think.
Got the message?

Once: Agriculture
Not so long ago: Industry
Now: Information
Tomorrow: Creativity
After that: Agriculture

Verb > To accompany Santiago Cirugeda's action as an architect we were looking for a similar critical action. Somebody who, from a position of knowledge of the media and the information society could perform a sort of alternative criticism, introducing new energy. Somebody who could postulate about the critical force that individuality can exert on a context in which any interactivity is possible. We thought of Geert Lovink and Arjen Mulder of the agency Bilwet/Adilkno (Foundation for the Advancement of Illegal Knowledge) and their activist texts, which they call UTOs (Unidentified Theoretical Objects). We proposed that they should interact with the content of Verb and so increase the multidisciplinarity of its production process.

Bilwet > Right, let's increase the complexity then, step by step, and radicalize the concept still further before business and mediocre academics, empty design and journalism can take over. These are the main enemies of any good journal.

Verb > Architecture is part of an everyday reality which the accelerated flow of information has turned into a combination of matter and information, of atoms and bytes, and which seems to allow for the development of informal or aleatory processes leading to multiple, subjective realities. Since architecture is based on a continuous reflection on and assimilation of this changing reality, *Verb* should collect and interpret signs of this process in and beyond traditional disciplinary limits.

Bilwet > Yes, and especially further develop the genre of the "architecture of networks," "net criticism" and "interface-network design," in a critical, practical and utopian sense. If you are clever, these days, you avoid the term "art." It could, instead, become a secret term, something of a positive taboo. There are so many entries in your story. Pick and choose, and don't worry too much about architecture as a discipline. I'm not very sure which way this first issue of *Verb* should go. Information and authorship. OK. That's a topic of the previous short summer of the internet, now in the process of being solved by copyright laws, lawyers, cops, big companies and clever software. It has a (guerrilla) war aspect. What else? Perhaps there are other ways of looking at it. For sure.

Is everyone a designer?[1]

Bilwet / Adilkno

DESIGNER MEDIA

To make a periodical, you need a format and a design. Then you just let volunteers and free-lancers fill up the columns; people that think they have something to say. A combination of design, marketing and distribution determines the success of the magazine. The content doesn't matter a fuck. But without content, the concept of the magazine degenerates into designer gloss, only interesting for professionals. The biggest danger for designer reviews is that the buyer will take the product for a professional journal. The empty look tells readers that they are completely free to ignore the content while enjoying the magazine. If they read it anyway, the word order is pure coincidence and the provocative quotes, sharp observations and intriguing associations are an extra added attraction. Design should be indeterminate and at the same time distinct. If the image is too strong, the whole thing will be perceived as lifestyle and design will have become fashion. As a useless product, design has to remain in the model stage to keep one step ahead of hype. It must constantly renew itself with software investment. When a program is understood, it can be thrown away. For centuries, the book was not marketed on the strength of its contents. The creative monks' designer Bibles weren't intended for reading, either. Church Latin had a nice typeface, but it was the pictures that made it ("Were the evangelists moonlighters?"). The male couple Gutenberg-Luther put an end to the *plaisir du texte*. Only in the era of designer media, in which words have been re-evaluated as random ASCII, has author-related content again become superfluous. The status of books and their authors' prestige vanish when you realize that they have to start moving in six weeks, and disappear from the shelves if they haven't moved in three months. To put a book on the shelves vertically is to declare it dead. The basic material called the 'book' has fallen into the hands of the window dresser. As soon as the book object stops presenting itself as a ware and avoids the *gesamtkunstwerk* of the bookstores, it has lost its scene and an unpredictable odyssey begins. The search for a title acquires a sporting aspect, and to read a title requires an 'uncontemporary' effort that can only be produced from behind a battery of answering machines, faxes, and turned-off doorbells. Once the designer book has shaken off its style, subject, author and market, it acquires the brilliance of a prodigy. Design speculates on the existence of an unknown that is discovered at the moment of design; it seeks not to exploit but to escape.

ACCURACY THROUGH OBSCURITY

The Net liberates the writer from his publisher. Unencumbered by resume or *oeuvre*, a willing author can hurl book after book directly onto the Net. If your masterpiece has been wiped off the newsgroups in ten days, you can park it on your own homepage, FTP-site, or BBS for the benefit of the virtual

---

{1} Johan Sjerpstra, "Virtual Writing. Everyone is a designer" in Adilkno, Media Archive. www.thing.desk.nl/bilwet/adilkno/themediaarchive

community. The writer can save her or his book from certain destruction in the paper market. The only thing that matters to the collection of connected are the tags. *'Weltfremdheit'* or 'discipline research' activates different search functions than 'Safe writing' or 'Ferdinand Kriwet' [2]. Electronic writers receive a daily, comprehensive literature update and this has consequences. Deconstruction software reveals which grammatical, rhetorical and educational tricks make a text readable in spite of its 'polculsex' [3] content. The quality of world literature is on the rise. If you follow the writing activities of renowned authors, the question of how they do it is quickly answered. It's a dizzying thought that earlier generations wrote their book with ineradicable ink. This is why programs are being developed on demand to produce text-critical editions during writing and send these tens of versions hourly to the fleet of hard discs that document culture in atomic shelters. To give their texts that little something extra that separates literature from the rest, authors throw their personality into the struggle, the unique combination of a gene-package, a cultural cross-over, salient biographical data and an education: Camilla Paglia, Donna Tart, Elisabeth Bronfen. The text that chooses to appear on the network instead of on the tablestrives for the greatest possible economy of the word. Reading pleasure used to be based on piling stylistic ornaments on top of story lines. The literary calculator now recognizes this to be static and an obstacle to communication. The electronic readers have all their texts pre-scanned, filtering out added value. For example, there is a killfile that destroys all sources and examples from 1989 (2012); a quotation eraser that gets rid of everything in quotes; the command 'skip interdisciplines', that erases everything expect the reader's specialization; 'create summary', that summarizes a text according to the reader's wishes; and 'show method', that shows self-referential excerpts and takes out all the exercises. 'Textual cleansing shareware' provides access to mega-*oeuvres* like Goethe, Simenon, Dilthey, Marx, Konsalik, Vestdijk, Balzac, Heidegger, Voltaire, D'Annunzio and Agatha Christie. A technical solution has been found for Althusser's guilt at not having read the complete Hegel and Kant. Human beings have a physical need to string words together striking the first hard sentence. At the end of the day, writing that makes use of the selection programs preserves the three sentences that withstood the test. Text production the following day starts with those three sentences. Less radical are the help files that remove mistakes, prevent platitudes and point out bad journalistic habits. The selection program removes all sentences using constructions such as "The eminent authority, would be justified in saying..." or italics that have been used to prop up weak sentences. The compact text naturally has the density of a summary, the quality of poetry, it conceals one's poor knowledge of foreign languages, suppresses every tendency towards explanation formalities and replaces the snail's pace of reason with the brilliance of the keyword. The point is to formulate knowledge so precisely and with such complexity that it cannot be hacked into by the software of others. Writing on computer must never reach a conclusion; if it did, the train of thought that produced it would have to be left out. Sentences no longer want to have a relationship with antecendent and offspring. Glue words like 'because', 'thus', 'as well as', and 'but' have been scrapped. In principle, any sentence may follow any other. The mystery of texts

{2} Radio-acoustic composer born in 1942 in Düsseldorf.
{3} Political, cultural, sexual.

is that an order of sentences does indeed exist. Text wants to be one step ahead of imagination and accelerates to the point of absurdity. It does not need the logic of machine language. One in a thousand texts contains something new; unlikely correspondences emerge (between the camera and a fish's eye, and what are Hindi-telephones?) that stimulate one's fantasy. Compressed text is precise and obscure. It evokes a hidden world of thought that seemingly need no longer be reported. People are becoming concrete, while the reader arrives at a level of abstraction that is usually inaccessible. Because EXIT signs have been hung all through the text, tourism in abstraction is easy to endure.

WRITING WITHOUT A CARRIER

Since ancient times, writing involved storage on clay tablets, parchment, paper or hard disk. Virtual writing means: producing language that only exists in the RAM. On-line text turns the written word into an unstable medium. There is no Nobel prize for the best telephone conversation. All of your love for humanity and genius is lost forever when you hang up. What the Hittites, Aztecs, Mayas and other vanished cultures talked about will remain a mystery to us. The written word causes single events. When text becomes as ephemeral as the spoken word, it ceases to be evidence. It does not need to preserve or transmit any culture. Context-free writing does not aim to retell any stories or to degenerate into a mythological stage. It practices the now-and-nevermore kind of communication and sharpens punctual consciousness. Language turns out to be capable of correctly transmitting the meanings we intend, when not distracted by body language or its setting. "When you narrow the bandwidth, you focus the message."

The real existing cyberspace of the chat boxes is still a text-based environment, not because of a cultural decision, but because of a technical limitation that people must live with at the end of the 1900's. The ephemeral computext is the ironic re-emergence of the written word after the word was declared dead in the new image culture. Writing has also succeeded in renewing itself by finding a new mass medium. All books can be resold anew on CD-ROM. The book store can survive, like the library annex databank. Melancholy warriors for the preservation of the written word should demand that all humanity go on-line as soon as possible. Literacy is learning to type on a keyboard, and large sections of the population must still be taught to express themselves through the keyboard. In the worldwide conspiracy, to avoid the convergence and synergy of mass and written culture, Sega and Nintendo have moved towards non-literary, visual interfaces, which require no command of language. "Text for some, images for all." The question is: is the Net to be a playground or a classroom? The speed with which Internet is spreading reveals the strength of text culture, until its take-over by television. Virtual writing is the written word's answer to the designer media, because it is not in search of a material form. It has already found one. The primitive nature of on-line text surpasses design. The ephemerality of real-time media negates all good intentions of stylists and curators. While text has been cornered by design in the paper world, it has created a new, free space in the electronic universe. Until the Net falls victim to the designers.

Coutras, not far from Bordeaux

Beginning of year 2000. The clients come from eastern France, where it's claimed the winters are both much harder and longer. In 1990 they found work in a vineyard in this part of the country and began living in a house rented from the proprietor. For several years their daughter lived with them before leaving to study in the city. Some time ago they decided to look for another house with more space in general, with more privacy and more land that would allow them to have a good-sized kitchen garden. But their salaries didn't stretch very far. First they looked at run-down country properties, which were prohibitive in relation to the time and money they'd have to invest to restore them. Next they began looking for a more modern house, with less space but easier to live in. But all these were variations on a single theme: standard houses with tiled roofs and 100 sqm of land, such as are seen in the outskirts of all French, and many European, towns; houses indifferent to the characteristics of the location they're in.

This is a phenomenon they don't understand. Why do people look for so much innovation in their cars and so little in their houses? Then the woman read an article about an exhibition on in Bordeaux in which <u>36 schemes by young teams of architects for houses costing a maximum of 500,000 francs</u> [€ 76.225] were being shown.

They went to see it, enjoyed themselves and, among many schemes that did no more than insist on the idea of a prototype, of repeating the same model – why? they ask, when it's been seen in repeated developments and estates of row-houses that these don't work –, they saw a house constructed on the outskirts of Bordeaux by some local architects that corresponded to what they were looking for. It had the appearance of a big greenhouse, with an opaque section facing the street and, on the garden side, an extended space with transparent outer wall conceived as a large terrace or winter garden. If the exhibition wasn't a fraud, why not ask the same architects to design a similar house for them? Despite the idea they had of architects – rich people, for wealthy clients –, they went to visit them. The construction work began in June, and was initially intended to be over by Christmas. Maybe this will be six months later.

The terrain is half of a partly urbanized, former farming property. The other half was sold at the same time to a family who also wanted to build a house on it.

Their works began soon afterwards, and they already live in it. It is a house of some 115 sqm that has come out at the same price as this one, which has 150 sqm of living space and the same amount again of winter garden or covered terrace. As the publicity for that monovolume says, "<u>What if the true luxury were space?</u>" While the works – which now mainly consist in co-producing the partitions and

HOUSE IN LA RENAUDERIE, Coutras (France)
<u>Architects</u>: Anne Lacaton & Jean Philippe Vassal. <u>Collaborators</u>: Emmanuelle
Delage, Sylvain Menaud, Christophe Hutin. <u>Clients</u>: Arlette Schwartz and Pierre
Guinchard. <u>Surface</u>: 290 sqm. <u>Cost</u>: € 64 790 tax excl. <u>Photographs</u>: Ramon
Prat. <u>Building system</u>: FILCLAIR 6,40 greenhouses: steel structure, transparent
ONEX glazing.

www.renault.com

interior wood finishes with a collaborator of the architects – advance, the rear section of the plot has already begun to assume the form of a kitchen garden, with its onions, garlic, tomatoes, potatoes, courgettes. On one side of this garden they have tried to set a small pine tree upright that had been blown over in the strong winds of Autumn 1999 and which is intended to become the regular Christmas tree. They will also plant flowers in the garden, but above all in the greenhouse: the winter garden. This is intended to be the setting for a large dining terrace that can be used all year round. On a sunny morning like today the outside temperature is some 6 degrees, and in the greenhouse it must be around 18 or 20. The partition walls and the roof of the house have to be completed. Maybe it's good to retain a vision of this sky from part of the main room.

Arlette and Pierre visited the *36 Propositions for a Home* exhibition at arc en rêve and saw there the Latapie House.

36 Propositions for a Home. Exhibition organized at arc en rêve, Bordeaux, and the book published by Périphériques and Birkhäuser.

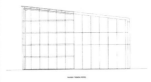

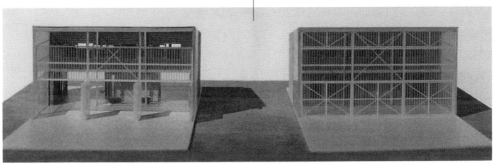

Latapie house. Lacaton & Vassal. Floriac, Bordeaux (1993).

LOCAUX / SURFACES EN M2	
SEJOUR	24,80
CUISINE	6,12
ENTREE	4,08
WC	1,53
ESCALIER	3,23
RANGT	1,44
CHAMBRE 1	14,00
CHAMBRE 2	24,00
S D B	4,05
DEGT./RANGT.	9,00
TOTAL	92,25
GARAGE/SEJOUR	14,00
SERRE/SEJOUR	63,00

LOT	PRIX FF HT/TTC
FONDATIONS/MAÇON.	44 595,00
CHARPENTE METAL	178 200,00
COUV./BARDAGE	14 300,00
PLOMBERIE SANITAIRE	20 685,00
ELEC./CHAUFFAGE	22 155,00
CLOISON/ISOLATION	18 457,00
MENUISERIE BOIS/ESC.	66 185,00
SOLS	5 250,00
TOTAL TRAVAUX HT	370 027,00
HONO. ARCHI. HT	44 403,00
TOTAL HT	414 430,00
TOTAL TTC	499 803,00

The plot of land is situated in the countryside, on the outskirts of Coutras, 50 km to the west of Bordeaux. This is an extremely long plot, having a frontage of 33 m along a local road. Part of the plot is classified as non-buildable agricultural land.

The surroundings are made up of scattered dwellings, cultivated farmland with occasional thickets of trees and bushes, and conglomerations of crop-growing greenhouses. The low density of vegetation and buildings and the flatness of the land encourage a wide-angle perception of the landscape in which the sky largely dominates.

In order to keep its distance from other houses and from the road, the house is set back some 30 m from the latter and on the very edge of the buildable area.

The house has only one floor, and it is made up of two juxtaposed and identical greenhouses. These are standard horticultural greenhouses, consisting of a metal framework and transparent rigid sheeting. They have the automatic features necessary for regulating their temperature, notably ventilation panels in the roof of each greenhouse, the opening of which is automated in relation to the indoor temperature. Approximately half the length of the facades can open by means of sliding doors. The rectangular plan, which runs north-south along the longer side of the plot, has two parts: the living areas – dining and family room, kitchen, bedrooms – are arranged on the west side in one of the greenhouses, and an open plan space – the winter garden – takes up the other greenhouse, on the east side.

The living areas open onto both the outside and the winter garden. Outside, the house will be supplemented by the planting of different fruit trees, forming an orchard.

On a sunny February morning like today the outside temperature is some 6 degrees, and in the greenhouse it must be around 18 or 20. The partition walls and the ceiling have to be completed. Maybe it would be good to retain a vision of this sky from part of the living room.

The clients have also undertaken an enormous amount of work in cleaning and preparing the plot, which is very large (5,500 sqm); they have lots of projects for this land.

They will also plant flowers in the garden, but above all in the greenhouse: the winter garden. This is intended to be the setting for a large dining terrace that can be used all year round.

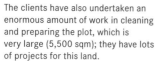

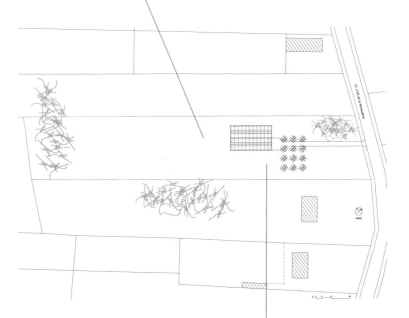

The house is set back some 30 m from the local road and on the very edge of the buildable area.

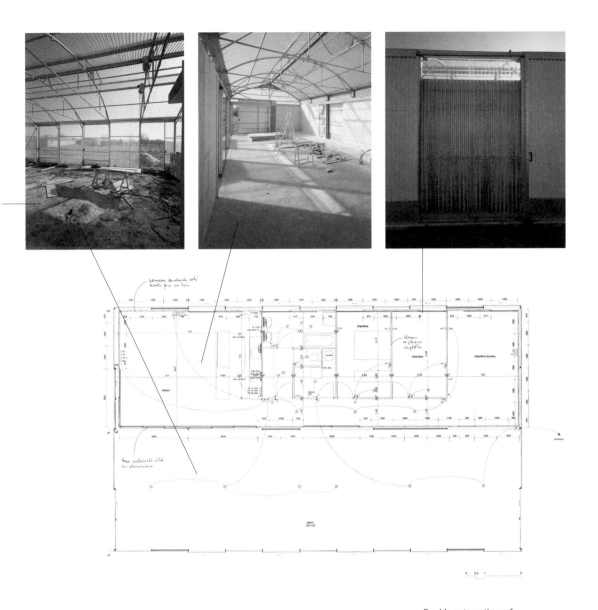

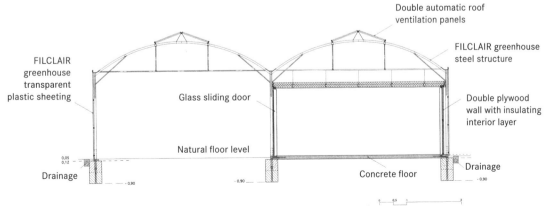

Double automatic roof
ventilation panels

FILCLAIR greenhouse
steel structure

FILCLAIR
greenhouse
transparent
plastic sheeting

Glass sliding door

Double plywood
wall with insulating
interior layer

Natural floor level

0,05
0,12

Drainage

Drainage

Concrete floor

- 0,90

- 0,90

- 0,90

Cross section

Anne Lacaton & Jean-Philippe Vassal > At first we opted for glass green-houses, but they are much more expensive, and at a certain moment the choice came up of either a 200 sqm house with glass greenhouses or a 300 sqm house with plastic ones.

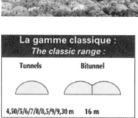

La gamme classique :
The classic range :

Tunnels   Bitunnel

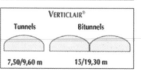

4,50/5/6/7/8/8,5/9/9,30 m   16 m

VERTICLAIR®

Tunnels   Bitunnels

7,50/9,60 m   15/19,30 m

It's a product we've been working on for a long time because we consider mass-produced greenhouses to be highly interesting, intelligent and beautiful constructions, and very cheap where such aspects are concerned.

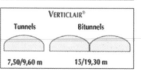

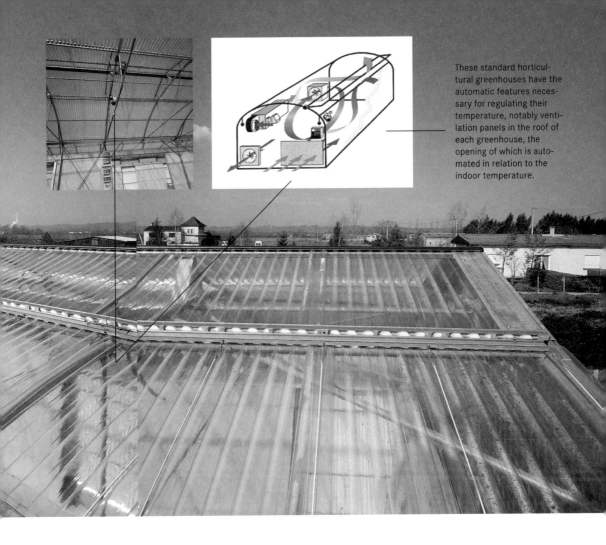

These standard horticultural greenhouses have the automatic features necessary for regulating their temperature, notably ventilation panels in the roof of each greenhouse, the opening of which is automated in relation to the indoor temperature.

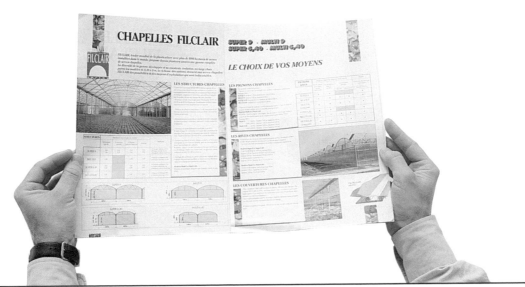

Lacaton-Vassal > Arlette and Pierre used to live in St Emilion in a rented house on the wine-producing estate where they work. They intended to leave this accommodation and for a while were looking for either an existing house to renovate or a plot of land to build a new house on as close as possible to their place of work.

They visited the *36 Propositions for a Home* exhibition at arc en rêve and saw the Latapie House. They got in touch with us straightaway to talk to us about their project. They were hesitant about the idea of constructing a new house. We met them, listened, then showed them the kind of work we do. They quickly became interested in our approach, in the idea of thinking about the largest, cheapest houses possible, evolving houses that use unusual building materials, in the idea of natural spaces and spaces of varying qualities in a house, of an openness towards the outside, etc.

These are people who are themselves capable of, and wish to, create things. We've found enough common points of interest (or of convergence) to take on the work on their house.

They hadn't, at the time, found the land. We thought this might take a while. We talked together about the qualities a site should have – mainly its situation with regard to sunlight or wind.

Two weeks later they called us because they'd seen a certain number of plots, and one in particular that pleased them. We went to see the land together. It was interesting because it's very flat, and you notice the sky above all else. On top of that it's very big. They subsequently bought this land, and we got down to work.

The idea of greenhouses soon came up, practically from the very first conversations. We'd spoken about these in relation to different projects, such as the Latapie House or the scheme for the university in Grenoble. It's a product we've been working on for a long time because we consider mass-produced greenhouses to be highly interesting, intelligent and beautiful constructions, and very cheap where such aspects are concerned.

The Coutras clients quickly grasped the idea that this system enabled large-size spaces to be constructed at low cost. They also liked the interior look they provide and the range of possibilities they offer.

The site on which the house resides enabled us to use the greenhouses without adapting them. On the one hand the system is very logical; on the other it's much more interesting to use them without any attempt at adaptation. It's a very well thought-out system of construction and, all things considered, rather beautiful. This is also a project we've wanted to do for a long time, and which has to do with the ideas we'd already worked on for the Latapie House (1st version).

At first we opted for glass greenhouses. But they are much more expensive, and at a certain moment the choice came up of either a 200 sqm house with glass greenhouses or a 300 sqm house with plastic ones. We visited different greenhouses with the clients, and they chose the second kind because finally they were taken with the idea of having more surface area. Generally speaking, we've worked a lot together on all the details of the scheme, so all the decisions have been taken in common. This is also because they've really been engaged with the project.

We designed, then, a scheme in which we commissioned a greenhouse manufacturer to construct two greenhouses with a total surface area of 300 sqm. We chose their location on the terrain and had the foundations made. The greenhouses have been built and we intervene subsequently in their interior to create the separate indoor features. These wood partitions are created by the clients, who wanted to participate in building something themselves. There are also outside contractors who intervene on the electricity, the plumbing and the glazed indoor partitions. It's a house that could be built very quickly if it was created all of a piece by various businesses. The clients have also undertaken an enormous amount of work in cleaning and preparing the plot, which is very large (5,500 sqm).

They have lots of projects for this land.

Sometimes the inhabitant manages to become, partly, the architect of his or her own home. Or at least the inhabitant manages to get involved in its production, in the same way as the architect tries to. Fundamentally, this is the idea around which the whole content of this issue revolves. We will continue along these lines in the next issue, analysing the relationship between information and the matter of construction. To what extent is built matter implemented on the basis of information? How is this development supposed to continue? See you again soon, in the next issue of *Verb* boogazine.

> VERB

Verb *Processing*, the first issue of Actar's boogazine, was produced by Jaime Salazar, Albert Ferré, Tomoko Sakamoto, Anna Tetas, Manuel Gausa (editors), Ramon Prat (editor, photographer and graphic designer), David Lorente and Anja Tränkel (graphic designers), Oriol Rigat, Carmen Galán and Leandro Linares (scanning and digital production), Paul Hammond, Tobias Willett, Felicity Gloth, Iñaki Ozkáriz and Kathy Lindstrom (translators), Dolors Soriano (technical production coordinator), Wanda Spangenberg (technical assistant), Ingoprint (printing), Cristina Lladó (press and public relations), and of course by all the people featured in this issue. We would like to thank them for their generosity and their patience, especially Alejandro Zaera-Polo, Farshid Moussavi and all of FOA's staff, Kunio Watanabe, Stefan Witteman, Tom Mossel, Eduardo Arroyo, Bernd Kniess, Manuel de Landa, Boštjan Vuga, Jurij Sadar, Anton Markus Pasing, Mark Jenewein, Thomas Pucher, Bernhard Schönherr, Helena and Hrvoje Njiric, Ira Koers and her partners at KZG, Santiago Cirugeda, Anne Lacaton, Jean Philippe Vassal, Arlette Schwartz and Pierre Guinchard. We thank as well the photographers who help to complement the architects' files and our own images: Stefan Schneider, Michael Raschke, Lukas Roth (b&k+), Jože Suhadolnik, Igor Omahen (Sadar & Vuga), Andreas Balon, Stefen Strassnig (LOVE) and Damir Fabijanic (njiric+njiric).

Our thanks also to:
The Information and Promotion Division of the General Affairs Bureau of the City of Yokohama. Makoto Fukuda and Kaori Sato for helping us understand the contents of the minutes of the Yokohama terminal meetings between the architects, the engineers, and the clients. Spela Mlakar, who introduced us to the work of Sadar Vuga Arhitekti and their Chamber of Commerce and Industry in Ljubljana. Darko Kramer for helping us understand the correspondence between njiric+njiric and the other parties involved in the construction of the Baumaxx hypermarket. Gabriele Hofer from ars electronica. Verónica Orueta from Tesauro for the Retevision advertisement video. Aaron Betsky, Nick Barley, Karl Chu, Tina Gregoric and Aljosa Dekleva, Cristina Díaz Moreno and Efrén García Grinda, Hans Magnus Enzensberger, Vicente Guallart, Michael Hensel, Sanford Kwinter, Arjen Mulder and Geert Lovink, Bartomeu Marí, Enric Monte, Ignasi Pérez Arnal, Juan Ramírez Guedes, Kelly Shannon, Akira Suzuki, Harm Tilman, Roemer van Toorn, Eyal Weizman and Joanna van der Zanden (and all of the do team) for their stimulating and guiding comments. Kazuhiro Kojima and Nobuaki Furuya for more stimulating ideas on architectural publishing shown in their Esquisse series of books published by Shokoku-sha, Tokyo. Sebastian Bissinger and Nikolai Wolff for all the energy and time they put into planning *Verb*'s still unscheduled launching events. And especially to Ricardo Devesa for the great initial push he gave to this publication.

Contact info:
ACTAR
Roca i Batlle 2
E-08023 Barcelona
www.actar.es
phone +34 934 187 759
fax +34 934 186 707
verb@actar-mail.com

Distributed by Actar
info@actar-mail.com

ISBN 84-95273-55-1
DL B-45322-2001
Printed and bound in the European Union
Barcelona, October 2001